DEVOTED TO WISDOM

CHOOSING WISDOM OR FOLLY

A 31 DAY DEVOTIONAL BASED ON THE BOOK OF PROVERBS

John E. Harrison, M.Div.

Good Tidings
goodtidings.com

DEDICATION

This book is dedicated to my lovely wife
and gift from God
Lynn Harrison
who has been
wholeheartedly behind me and supportive of me
in the inception of and writing of this book in its entirety.
Thank you!

ACKNOWLEDGEMENTS

A very big thank you goes out to my brother, Arthur Harrison
for his many hours given to the proofreading of this book
and for his suggestions and ideas which have added greatly to its clarity.
We have been through a lot together in this!
Thank you!

Thank you also to the many people in my church who have helped make this a reality.
Thank you to my pastor for his time and effort in reviewing this book!
Thank you to the members of our worship team for being a sounding board every week!
Thank you to others who have invested in this book! May you be blessed by God!

Finally, thank you, perhaps posthumously at this point, to my seventh grade English instructor,
Mr. McLoughlin, for instilling in me an interest in, and a love for, writing books.
I still remember you drawing a picture of a pipe on the blackboard
to illustrate prepositions: through the pipe, over the pipe, on/in the pipe, around the pipe!
Never end a sentence with one of those prepositions!
Then you drew smoke coming out of the pipe, left it there for 5 seconds, smiled at us,
erased it, then put a picture of it on our exam and asked us to finish the picture for extra points!
I did! Oh, those were the days! You named your classes by sports teams. We were the Red Sox!
I still remember. Thank you!

PREFACE

This book is a devotional based upon the book of Proverbs, which was written by Solomon, the new King of Israel, succeeding his father, King David. Solomon is now passing along wisdom, which he has gained from God and from life, to his son Rehoboam, and to his daughters, but especially to his son.

This book is written as a devotional. As such, the format will appear as: Scripture, Devotion, Commentary, Scripture, followed by Prayer. I am not expecting the reader to pray these prayers. I am not ritualistic, nor am I a fan of recited prayers. I am offering these prayers as I write. Day 2 will include a 'we' prayer, but again, I am offering this prayer as I write, and do not expect the reader to pray it.

All Scripture quoted is taken from the 8/28/2019 World English Bible. In this translation, the word 'prudence' will appear. Good synonyms that I would suggest would be wisdom (of course), along with discretion, coolness, and carefulness. The word Yahweh will also appear, frequently, being the Hebrew word for God. If you are more comfortable with other Names, you may use such as: Lord, LORD, or Jehovah.

There are 'Easter eggs' scattered throughout this book. You may find your favorite hymn here, or song, even a seasonal song, perhaps your favorite cartoon or movie character, or even your favorite place to visit. If they are in the public domain, they will be easy to spot. If not, the reference to such may be vague, or a name may even be spelled differently. See how many you can find! Enjoy!

I have shared important journeys in my life throughout this book, along with wisdom that I have picked up along the way, in my life and in my Christian walk. I pass these along to share with you.

In writing this devotional, it is my prayer as the writer that we will gain wisdom in making good choices in life. May God guide us and grant us wisdom as we take this journey together. In Jesus' Name. Amen!

Proverbs 1:1

The proverbs of Solomon, the son of David, king of Israel

Proverbs 1:2-7

2 to know wisdom and instruction;
    to discern the words of understanding;
3 to receive instruction in wise dealing,
    in righteousness, justice, and equity;
4 to give prudence to the simple,
    knowledge and discretion to the young man:
5 that the wise man may hear, and increase in learning;
    that the man of understanding may attain to sound counsel:
6 to understand a proverb, and parables,
    the words and riddles of the wise.
7 The fear of Yahweh is the beginning of knowledge;
    but the foolish despise wisdom and instruction.

Wisdom, Day 1. The Beginning Of Knowledge

I am one who grew up in church, from the nursery all the way up through grade school and beyond, into adulthood, and right up to the present day. I have always been one who went to church. I began in Sunday school, in the First Church of Marlborough, Massachusetts, in the 1950s. I grew up with 2 brothers, 1 younger and 1 older. Our parents brought us to church every Sunday, dropped us off at Sunday school, and then went upstairs to the sanctuary, as both Sunday school and worship met at the same time. Then they picked us up at the conclusion of the service and we drove home. My parents were amazed at my ability to recite Scripture that I had learned in Sunday school as we drove home, especially **John 3:16**. However, it would not be until age 13 that that Scripture would take on a personal meaning for me in my life, when I would come to know in my heart Who Jesus is.

I began writing this devotional with the premise that in every case throughout the Biblical book of Proverbs, wherever and whenever the word wisdom is used, the word may be replaced with the Name of Jesus. To know wisdom is to know Jesus. To ask for wisdom is to ask for Jesus. To get Jesus is to get wisdom. It soon became apparent that there was another player in this story, Folly. It will become apparent that Folly represents the Devil, or Satan. For now, this will simply be the premise. It should become clear by Proverbs 6 that this is so. The reader is simply asked at this point to go along with, and consider this as a premise for now, and hopefully come on board by Proverbs 6.

To begin, there is a difference between head knowledge and heart knowledge. There is a difference between those who know Who Jesus is with head knowledge and those who know Jesus with their heart from a personal walk with Him.

John 7:28-29. Jesus therefore cried out in the temple, teaching and saying, "You both know me, and know where I am from. I have not come of myself, but he who sent me is true, whom you don't know. I know him, because I am from him, and he sent me."

Prayer. Lord God, as we begin this study, we do so because we have a desire to know wisdom and instruction. Teach us, I pray, by Your Holy Spirit, Who You are, and what You would have us learn. May we learn from You as we begin this study. We want to know wisdom. We want to know You. For the fool has said in his heart, there is no God. We want to be wise. We want to be followers of You, Lord. Teach us, I pray. In Jesus' Name. Amen.

Proverbs 1:20-26

20 Wisdom calls aloud in the street.
>She utters her voice in the public squares.

21 She calls at the head of noisy places.
>At the entrance of the city gates, she utters her words:

22 "How long, you simple ones, will you love simplicity?
>How long will mockers delight themselves in mockery,
>and fools hate knowledge?

23 Turn at my reproof.
>Behold, I will pour out my spirit on you.
>I will make known my words to you.

24 Because I have called, and you have refused;
>I have stretched out my hand, and no one has paid attention;

25 but you have ignored all my counsel,
>and wanted none of my reproof;

26 I also will laugh at your disaster.
>I will mock when calamity overtakes you.

Wisdom, Day 2. The Call Of Wisdom

There is a reason that opponents of God and of Christianity want all forms thereof removed and no longer be displayed in public places. They oppose manger scenes, crosses, the Ten Commandments, and all such displays in public places. Merry Christmas has been replaced by Happy Holidays for a reason. It is in these places that Jesus cries aloud to warn us of our strayings and to lead us in the ways that we should go. These actions are offensive to those who want to go their own way.

It used to be that town squares were owned and maintained by churches and that was where the business of the town took place, intermingling the two together. I grew up in Marlborough, Massachusetts, and attended church at the First Church in Marlborough. That church owns and maintains the town square and has done so since both were founded in the early 1660s. On that property sits the John Brown Bell, a symbol of the anti-slavery movement of the mid-1800s. The bell was seized in 1859, brought to Marlborough, and used as a bell on the town's fire apparatus. When this use became outgrown, the bell was then put on display in a bell tower on the town square. The citizens of Harper's Ferry in West Virginia still want the bell to be returned. But the bell is alarmed and has remained on the church's property.

Jesus taught openly in public places, in the Temple, among crowds of people.

John 18:20. (Jesus) "I spoke openly to the world. I always taught in synagogues, and in the temple, where the Jews always meet. I said nothing in secret."

He has commanded us to proclaim His Word from the housetops.

Matthew 10:27. What I tell you in the darkness, speak in the light; and what you hear whispered in the ear, proclaim on the housetops.

It is appropriate then, for Jesus to call aloud outside, to raise His voice in the open squares, to cry aloud in the chief concourses, and at the openings of the gates in the city. It was at those places that the business of the city was conducted. How unfortunate that our society seeks to silence that voice. It must be heard! We are to be that voice.

2 Chronicles 7:14. if my people, who are called by my name, will humble themselves, pray, seek my face, and turn from their wicked ways, then I will hear from heaven, will forgive their sin, and will heal their land.

Prayer. Lord God, we confess before You the forgivable sins of our country and repent of them, freeing ourselves of the consequences of sin. Forgive us of our forgivable sins, I pray. Teach us, oh Lord, to proclaim Your Word once again, even in the dark, among the people, and even from the housetops. Enable ears to hear once again, I pray. Hear from Heaven, oh Lord, forgive our sins, and heal our land. In Jesus' Name. Amen.

Proverbs 1:23

Turn at my reproof.
>Behold, I will pour out my spirit on you.
>I will make known my words to you.

Wisdom, Day 3. Spirit Poured Out

I graduated from college, earning a Bachelor of Arts degree in religion, and graduated from seminary, with a Master of Divinity degree, and somehow no one told me about the baptism of the Holy Spirit, or acquainted me with the third person of the Trinity. In all fairness, the college that I attended is open to people of all faiths and the seminary that I attended is an interdenominational school. So perhaps that is not so surprising. After graduating from both schools and being in ministry for several years, I returned home to wait upon the Lord for further direction in my life. A wonderful country preacher, there and then, took it upon himself to acquaint my family and me with the Holy Spirit. While I was attending a Bible study at my parents' house, I was invited to lay hands on, and pray for, an older brother in the Lord. As I was praying, I felt a tingling come upon me, and as I prayed, words began to come out of my mouth that were not my own. I spoke, albeit briefly, in another language, a prayer language, and felt power going forth from me, yet that was not coming from me, that was present for the healing of my elder brother. I became empowered that night for the ministry that I had begun. Power! Up to this point, my ministry had been weak and without real power. The Holy Spirit that Jesus had promised had been poured out upon me…upon…me! God loved me so much that He poured out His Holy Spirit upon me, for the purpose of empowering the ministry to which He had called me.

This is what Jesus promised.

John 14:6. (Jesus) "I am the way, the truth, and the life. No one comes to the Father, except through me."

This is what God promised.

Acts 2:17. "It will be in the last days", says God,
> "that I will pour out my Spirit on all flesh.
> Your sons and your daughters will prophesy.
> Your young men will see visions.
> Your old men will dream dreams."

This is what was prophesied.

Joel 2:28. "It will happen afterward, that I will pour out my Spirit on all flesh;
> and your sons and your daughters will prophesy.
> Your old men will dream dreams.
> Your young men will see visions."

Amazing! From that point forward, whenever I read God's Word, it comes alive for me! New and clearer meaning seems to almost jump off the written page for me. God's Word is made known to me! I can't imagine now having done ministry before, without the empowerment of God's Holy Spirit.

Wisdom says, surely, I will pour out my spirit on you; I will make my words known unto you. Folly, we will find, is in it for herself, for what she can get out of it, and offers nothing in return. The choice seems clear and simple to me. I have chosen Wisdom. I have instructed my children to choose Wisdom. I continue to choose Wisdom. Today and every day.

Prayer. Father, thank You for giving us free will, the ability to choose for ourselves. What a precious gift You have given unto us. You could have created us as mindless, obedient servants. But You chose to give us the gift of free will. Thank You, Father! Teach us now to choose wisely, I pray, this day and always. May we choose Wisdom and reject Folly. Always! In Jesus' Name. Amen!

Proverbs 1:24-33

24 Because I have called, and you have refused;
    I have stretched out my hand, and no one has paid attention;
25 but you have ignored all my counsel,
    and wanted none of my reproof;
26 I also will laugh at your disaster.
    I will mock when calamity overtakes you;
27 when calamity overtakes you like a storm,
    when your disaster comes on like a whirlwind;
    when distress and anguish come on you.
28 Then will they call on me, but I will not answer.
    They will seek me diligently, but they will not find me;
29 because they hated knowledge,
    and didn't choose the fear of Yahweh.
30 They wanted none of my counsel.
    They despised all my reproof.
31 Therefore they will eat of the fruit of their own way,
    and be filled with their own schemes.
32 For the backsliding of the simple will kill them.
    The careless ease of fools will destroy them.
33 But whoever listens to me will dwell securely,
    and will be at ease, without fear of harm.

Wisdom, Day 4. Choosing Wisdom Or Folly

My favorite movie of all time was made just after the Great Depression and was one of the first to use the new technology of filming in color. It starred a self-proclaimed wise man of his bright green city. It also starred a young girl who spent most of the movie and her adventure trying to get back home. She was the girl in the gingham dress. We'll call her Daura T. Upon her arrival in her dream land, she meets the two protagonists of the movie. We'll call them the Protector of the North and the Harasser of the West. Daura T. has a choice to make, as to which one of these two women she is going to listen to and trust in her adventure. Will she trust in her Protector, or will she give in to pressure and appease her Harasser? They both have powers beyond those of her own and she finds herself in many difficult situations. She meets friends along the way, all of whom need help as well, and they band together, resist the Harasser, and trust the Protector. Throughout her adventure, Daura T. holds on tightly to that which the Harasser wants and does not give in to pressure. She makes many choices throughout her adventure, and through persistence and help she and her friends have their needs met. By a conscious choice to resist their Harasser and trust their Protector, her friends have their needs met and Daura T. makes it home!

We were created with a free will, to choose to do as we wish. Those of us who are fortunate enough to live in the United States of America are privileged to live in a free society, enjoying many freedoms, such as those of speech, press, and religion, to name a few. Along with those freedoms comes responsibility, such as respecting one another's rights and freedoms and obeying the laws of the land.

Proverbs 16:9. A man's heart plans his course,
          but Yahweh directs his steps.

John 7:17. (Jesus) "If anyone desires to do his will, he will know about the teaching, whether it is from God, or if I am speaking from myself."

We are given a choice, as to whether or not we will accept the pursuit of Wisdom. With that choice comes certain freedoms, but also certain responsibilities and consequences. We are told here that if we listen to Wisdom, or Jesus, we will dwell securely and will be at ease, without fear of harm. The choice is ours; we are free to choose and follow as we see fit. But consequences will follow. I advise us to choose wisely. The choice seems quite clear and simple to me. I chose, and continue to choose daily, to follow Wisdom and Jesus. I made that choice at the young age of 13 years and have never regretted it. I have found that I dwell securely and am at ease, without fear of harm.

Prayer. Lord, I pray that You will continue to honor the choice that I have made in life and honor Your Word. I pray that my readers will also choose wisely, that they have listened, and will listen, to Your voice, choose Jesus, and that we may follow Him faithfully all the days of our lives. For as for me and my house, we will choose the Lord. In Jesus' Name. Amen!

Proverbs 1:33, 4:6-9

1:33 But whoever listens to me will dwell securely,
and will be at ease, without fear of harm.
4:6 Don't forsake her, and she will preserve you.
Love her, and she will keep you.
7 Wisdom is supreme.
Get wisdom.
Yes, though it costs all your possessions, get understanding.
8 Esteem her, and she will exalt you.
She will bring you to honor, when you embrace her.
9 She will give to your head a garland of grace.
he will deliver a crown of splendor to you.

Wisdom, Day 5. Security

During my college years, I worked in a summer town in southern Maine. Every year, just before Memorial Day, I would leave Kentucky, return to New England, and spend my summers in a beach town in Maine working in restaurants. My life changed in 1979. The restaurant where I had been working closed, and the owner sold it to someone else. My dad had retired and had taken a job as a security guard for a local computer company. I was now attending seminary in Massachusetts, so I chose to work as a security guard, along with my dad. I took to the security business quickly, like a duck to water. I took security seriously, making it my responsibility to protect the building in which I was working, along with the people who worked there. I avoided the stereotype of the position. I did not sleep, or even doze, on duty. I would not even take a 'turn-around' shift, going home at midnight and returning at 8:00 am, or even take a double shift, at least not voluntarily, as I did not think that I would be alert enough to do my job safely. My boss took note of this, being concerned at first. If I was working a midnight to morning shift, he would call me at 7:00 am, and make sure that I was alert for those coming in to work and for the changing of the guard. But eventually he knew that he could trust me and promoted me to the position of guarding the main, flagship building. Security became a part of who I was. Safety, security, and protection, then, are important to me and it means a lot to me that Wisdom offers these traits: "Whoever listens to me will dwell securely."

Proverbs 14:26. In the fear of Yahweh is a secure fortress,
and he will be a refuge for his children.

Jesus offers us these same qualities and protections.

Psalm 46:1. God is our refuge and strength,
a very present help in trouble.

Jeremiah 29:11. "For I know the thoughts that I think toward you", says Yahweh, "thoughts of peace, and not of evil, to give you hope and a future."

2 Thessalonians 3:3. But the Lord is faithful, who will establish you, and guard you from the evil one.

We have security, safety, and preservation in Wisdom then, as well as in Jesus. These are good places in which to live and dwell.

As rings true in the old hymn by Elisha A. Hoffman:
Leaning, leaning,
Safe and secure from all alarms;
Leaning, leaning,
Leaning on the Everlasting Arms.

The choice is ours to make. We have a free will to choose, a gift from God. We may choose to accept His offer of protection or refuse it. How will we respond?

I choose to accept His offer and His gift, freely, gladly.

Prayer. Thank You, Lord, that You are our Protector. Teach us to trust in You, that we may dwell securely in You. In Jesus' Name. Amen.

Proverbs 2:1-15

1 My son, if you will receive my words,
    and store up my commandments within you;
2 So as to turn your ear to wisdom,
    and apply your heart to understanding;
3 Yes, if you call out for discernment,
    and lift up your voice for understanding;
4 If you seek her as silver,
    and search for her as for hidden treasures:
5 then you will understand the fear of Yahweh,
    and find the knowledge of God.
6 For Yahweh gives wisdom.
    Out of his mouth comes knowledge and understanding.
7 He lays up sound wisdom for the upright.
    He is a shield to those who walk in integrity;
8 that he may guard the paths of justice,
    and preserve the way of his saints.
9 Then you will understand righteousness and justice,
    equity and every good path.
10 For wisdom will enter into your heart.
    Knowledge will be pleasant to your soul.
11 Discretion will watch over you.
    Understanding will keep you,
12 to deliver you from the way of evil,
    from the men who speak perverse things;
13 who forsake the paths of uprightness,
    to walk in the ways of darkness;
14 who rejoice to do evil,
    and delight in the perverseness of evil;
15 who are crooked in their ways,
    and wayward in their paths.

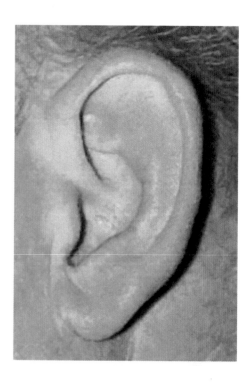

Wisdom, Day 6. The Value Of Wisdom

Incline your ear to Jesus. Listen to Jesus. I begin each day by listening to Jesus, listening for the still, small voice of the Lord. I spend some quiet time listening, really listening, tuning out the world, shutting off the computer, putting down the devices, being quiet before the Lord, and listening, really listening. For I usually do not find the voice of the Lord to be audible, or to be a loud, booming voice, easily discernible, easily recognizable; but rather I usually find it to be more likely a still, small voice, one that I have to really listen to in order to hear. I find it preferable to listen during the early part of the day, before I've become distracted by the busyness of my schedule and by those things that are competing for my attention and need to be tended. I may hear the voice of Jesus as I'm reading from God's Word as I begin my day. I may hear the voice of Jesus in the lyrics of a song being played during my morning devotions or commute. Or, I may hear the voice of Jesus as I just be still and listen for His still, small voice. I have found that I need to get up a little earlier in the morning so that after listening to my praise music, reading God's Word, and spending time in prayer, I can just sit quietly for a little while longer and listen quietly for Jesus to speak to me. After doing this for some time, I know the voice of Jesus and am able to discern His voice from other voices that I may be hearing.

John 10:27. "My sheep hear my voice, and I know them, and they follow me."

1 Kings 19:11-12. (Yahweh) "Go out, and stand on the mountain before Yahweh." Behold, Yahweh passed by, and a great and strong wind tore the mountains, and broke in pieces the rocks before Yahweh; but Yahweh was not in the wind. After the wind there was an earthquake; but Yahweh was not in the earthquake. After the earthquake a fire passed; but Yahweh was not in the fire. After the fire, there was a still small voice.

Psalm 46:10. "Be still, and know that I am God.
          I will be exalted among the nations.
          I will be exalted in the earth."

The Lord gives Jesus.

John 3:16a. For God so loved the world, that he gave his one and only Son…

It doesn't say that God loved us so much that He said, "I love you!" No! It's not about what we say; it's about what we do. For God so loved the world that He gave…Jesus!

When Jesus enters our heart, He preserves us. He keeps us. He will deliver us from the way of evil.

John 17:12b,c; 18:9b. Those whom you have given me I have kept. None of them is lost.

God never promised any one of us that we would have an easy, comfortable stroll down a well-mown garden path, although that is what I often want and many of us want. He promises to walk with us.

Prayer. Lord God, teach us to listen each day to Your still, small voice. May we know the depth of Your love for us. Teach us, Lord, to walk in the way that You would have us to go. Lead us, I pray. We will follow. In Jesus' Name. Amen!

Proverbs 2:16-17

16 To deliver you from the strange woman,
  even from the foreigner who flatters with her words;
17 who forsakes the friend of her youth,
  and forgets the covenant of her God.

Wisdom, Day 7. The Perils Of Folly

During my college years, I spent my summer months in a beach town. When the weather was nice, I spent my mornings on the beach and my afternoons working. I was young, and still single. I liked to play frisbee at the time and would often bring my frisbee down to the beach with me and practice throwing my frisbee by myself. I would throw it diagonally up into the air, it would come back down to me, I would catch it, and throw it back up into the air again. On one particular day, a girl who was about my age, and was clad in a lime sherbet green bikini, invited herself into my game of frisbee. She seemed to be quite adept at the sport and we spent about half an hour throwing my frisbee to each other. It was an enjoyable pastime, but work soon beckoned. We exchanged pleasantries and went our separate ways. I returned to the beach on the following day and wouldn't you know it, she was there again and invited herself into my game once again. It turned out that she was a nurse at the local hospital and spent her mornings on the beach as well. My mother cautioned me against her, with the words, "Make sure that's all that she wants." I did not know what she meant, being young and naïve; we were just enjoying passing the time with a game of frisbee. We did so on several more days. Then, on one particular day, I chose to ride my bike instead of going down to the beach. Perhaps it was too cool for the beach, I don't remember why. But as I was riding my bike, I saw my beach companion sitting in a parked car with another man, drinking a beer. I knew then that my mother was right. This was not the woman in whom I should be interested. I was not the only guy she was spending time. I never saw her again that summer. Perhaps she had noticed that I had seen her with another man, I don't know. September soon came and I went back to college. I returned the next summer, but I never saw her again.

In this passage of Scripture, we are introduced to Folly, who is described as an immoral woman, a seductress, who flatters us with her words. At some point in the early part of her life she had a companion, but she has since forsaken her companion and has forgotten the covenant of her God.

Folly is pursuing many interests. She was once married, but has forsaken the companion, or husband, of her youth. She is an adulterous woman. She has also forgotten the covenant of her God. She is attempting to seduce those whom she seeks out and flatters them with her words. She has gone astray and is seeking to lead others astray with her.

In God's instructions to Joshua for entering into Canaan, the Promised Land, He said,

Joshua 1:2b, 7b. "Go across this Jordan, you and all these people, to the land which I am giving to them, even to the children of Israel…Don't turn from it to the right hand or to the left, that you may have good success wherever you go."

In the Sermon on the Mount, Jesus says,

Matthew 7:13-14. "Enter in by the narrow gate; for the gate is wide and the way is broad that leads to destruction, and there are many who enter in by it. How the gate is narrow and the way is restricted that leads to life! There are few who find it."

Prayer. Lord, thank You for this warning. Teach us to choose our way carefully. Teach us not to go by the same way that many choose, but teach us to choose carefully, for You are the Way, the Truth, and the Life. Draw us unto You, oh Lord, and teach us to follow You, all the days of our lives. In Jesus' Name. Amen!

Proverbs 2:18-19

18 For her house leads down to death,
    her paths to the departed spirits.
19 None who go to her return again,
    neither do they attain to the paths of life.

Wisdom, Day 8. Folly Leads To Death

I was hiking along a mountain trail one day, up Cadillac Mountain, in Bar Harbor, Maine. It is not a very high mountain, the peak of which is only at 1,532 feet, but it is the highest point along the North Atlantic seaboard. During my ascent, I strayed off of the marked trail. I had been following white arrows along the trail, but I noticed that I hadn't seen any of these in some time and the hike was becoming more difficult. Finally, my ascent had become more vertical than my comfort allowed, and it was now more of a climb than a hike. However, unwilling to admit that I had lost the trail, I continued to climb. I rationalized that I was going up, making progress, and I would at some point find and rejoin the actual trail. However, I had to admit that continuing was becoming hazardous. Rocks were slipping out from under my feet, and keeping my footing was becoming challenging. I finally reached a ledge upon which I could stand and pondered my next move. I decided to hike horizontally off to the left to see if I could regain the path. Trees and brush only got thicker and my spirit told me that I had to turn back. I reversed my climb, which was not an easy task, and returned to the point where I had strayed from the path. I looked around carefully and saw a narrow passage between two clumps of trees. There I saw two white arrows that I had missed, pointing further up the mountain. Passing through this gap in the clump of trees, I found that the trail did indeed continue from this point. I continued along the trail, the ascent was much easier, and I soon reached the summit. Wisdom had delivered me from my foolishness and protected me from harm and perhaps even death, if I had lost my footing on my difficult climb.

Be warned! Following after Folly leads to death! Do not walk along the same path with her, for her path leads to the dead. It is a busy, dead end street. There are many who walk upon it. Do not choose to go the way of the many! Folly's house is not just a house, but a way. Many choose it. Beware!

The parallel here to Lucifer is too clear to be a coincidence and I submit that he is represented here. Lucifer was the crown prince of Heaven. He rebelled against God, was cast out of Heaven, and thrown down to Earth. We now know Lucifer by his fallen name, Satan, or the Devil, whose ultimate fate is the Lake of Fire, or death, or Hell.

It makes sense to me to avoid her then, at all costs, and to avoid the Devil, whom Folly represents.

Revelation 20:10. The devil who deceived them was thrown into the lake of fire and sulfur, where the beast and the false prophet are also. They will be tormented day and night forever and ever.

That is a long time, forever. There is no reprieve; there is no escape. There will be no movie about it, starring the man of many names. There will be no finding a way out of there.

The Devil is trying to pull as many of God's people down with him as he can. Following him leads to the same death. I submit that Folly represents the Devil, who is competing with Wisdom, Jesus, for our attention and affections. Folly's offer may look appealing at first, as there is pleasure in sin, but for a season. Who will we choose, then, Wisdom or Folly? Again, the choice seems clear to me.

Joshua 24:15. "If it seems evil to you to serve Yahweh, choose today whom you will serve…but as for me and my house, we will serve Yahweh."

Hebrews 11:24-26. By faith, Moses…refused to be called the son of Pharaoh's daughter, choosing rather to share ill treatment with God's people than to enjoy the pleasures of sin for a time, considering the reproach of Christ greater riches than the treasures of Egypt; for he looked to the reward.

Prayer. Lord, we are faced with a choice today as to who we will follow, Wisdom or Folly, Jesus or the Devil. Grant us Wisdom, Lord, that we may choose wisely. Teach us to follow after You, Lord, all the days of our lives. May we never leave You nor forsake You. Lead us, Lord. In Jesus' Name. Amen.

Proverbs 3:13-26

13 Happy is the man who finds wisdom,
    the man who gets understanding.
14 For her good profit is better than getting silver,
    and her return is better than fine gold.
15 She is more precious than rubies.
    None of the things you can desire are to be compared to her.
16 Length of days is in her right hand.
    In her left hand are riches and honor.
17 Her ways are ways of pleasantness.
    All her paths are peace.
18 She is a tree of life to those who lay hold of her.
    Happy is everyone who retains her.
19 By wisdom Yahweh founded the earth.
    By understanding, he established the heavens.
20 By his knowledge, the depths were broken up,
    and the skies drop down the dew.
21 My son, let them not depart from your eyes.
    Keep sound wisdom and discretion:
22 so they will be life to your soul,
    and grace for your neck.
23 Then you shall walk in your way securely.
    Your foot won't stumble.
24 When you lie down, you will not be afraid.
    Yes, you will lie down, and your sleep will be sweet.
25 Don't be afraid of sudden fear,
    neither of the desolation of the wicked, when it comes:
26 for Yahweh will be your confidence,
    and will keep your foot from being taken.

Wisdom, Day 9. Guidance For The Young

One of the first things that a new Christian might say, after making a decision to accept Jesus Christ as their Lord and Savior, is, "I found Jesus!" That statement seems to be confusing to many, to Christians and non-Christians alike. Although a non-Christian may not understand what that means, it can be confusing to a Christian as well. What does that statement really mean? Did the person make the effort all on their own, and even though they were lost in their sin and their eyes were blinded, they found Jesus? Certainly, Jesus wasn't lost somewhere, and that person happened along the way, found Jesus, and returned Him to the Father. Yet that could be a logical deduction from that statement.

John 15:16a. (Jesus) "You didn't choose me, but I chose you, and appointed you."

When Zacchaeus climbed the sycamore tree to see Jesus, Jesus stood at the base of the tree, looked up and said,

Luke 19:5b. "Zacchaeus, hurry and come down…"

Zacchaeus thought he was looking for Jesus, but Jesus was looking for Zacchaeus. It is Jesus who seeks us and calls us.

John 14:6. (Jesus) "I am the way, the truth, and the life. No one comes to the Father, except through me."

Yet, from our point of view, how much happier we are when we 'find Jesus' and follow Him.

We probably all have our favorite place on Earth to sit and gaze upon the wonder of God's Creation. My all-time favorite place to just sit and gaze wonderingly is at the rim of the Grand Canyon, in Arizona. I could sit there for hours on end and just stare into the ever-changing colors of the canyon walls. And as I do so, I see the fingerprints of God in His handiwork. Somehow, I just know that Jesus had a hand in the making of it all.

John 1:1-3. In the beginning was the Word, and the Word was with God, and the Word was God. The same was in the beginning with God. All things were made through him. Without him was not anything made that has been made.

The Word is Jesus. All things in God's Creation were made through Jesus. He is the Creator.

Has anyone ever asked you, "Are you still doing that church thing?" "Haven't you done that long enough?" Yes, I'm still doing that church thing! It's called the Christian walk and I'm in it for the long haul. I've been walking this walk all of my life. I grew up in church, from the nursery all the way up, and I never left. This is a lifetime commitment for me. No, I haven't been doing it long enough. I plan to keep on walking the Christian walk for the rest of my life.

1 Corinthians 9:24. Don't you know that those who run in a race all run, but one receives the prize? Run like that, that you may win.

The prize that we are to obtain is eternal life, eternity with Jesus. To hear, "Well done, good and faithful servant" (**Matthew 25:21**), we must finish the race. Keep Jesus! Hang on. Do not let go.

John 15:4. (Jesus) "Remain in me, and I in you. As the branch can't bear fruit by itself, unless it remains in the vine, so neither can you, unless you remain in me."

Prayer. Thank You, Father, for the wonder of Your Creation and for choosing us. Teach us to walk with You, today and always. In Jesus' Name. Amen.

Proverbs 3:16-17

16 Length of days is in her right hand.
  In her left hand are riches and honor.
17 Her ways are ways of pleasantness.
  All her paths are peace.

Wisdom, Day 10. Blessings

I have been blessed with youthful looks for most of my life. People have asked me, "John, what's your secret? How do you look so young?" Do you want to know my answer? I honored my mother and my father according to the Ten Commandments. This commandment comes with a promise:

Exodus 20:12. Honor your father and your mother, that your days may be long in the land which Yahweh your God gives you.

People have had difficulty believing me when I tell them my age. Youth, and the ability to take part in the activities that come with it, have followed me for most of my life. It is only now, that I am in my 60s, that dark blonde hair has given way to that of gray, and now even beginning to turn to white. But those are the colors of wisdom! Ah, length of days. I am beginning to struggle with that now, in the later years of my life, especially with medical diagnoses. My wife has held on to me and told me, "I don't want you to die, or to get sick!" God's response:

Ezekiel 18:32. "For I have no pleasure in the death of him who dies," says the Lord Yahweh. "Therefore, turn yourselves, and live."

Isn't that a precious promise? In my recent health struggles, God caused our guitarist at church to fall down on his knees before Him, put his hand on the place of my pain, and pray tearfully for my healing! God is honoring that prayer! Healing is taking place in me, even as I press on to write this book, while I still have time. God is healing me! Amen! Riches and honor? Not so much. Solomon got that deal.

2 Chronicles 1:10-12. (Solomon) "Now give me wisdom and knowledge, that I may go out and come in before this people; for who can judge this great people of yours?"

God said to Solomon, "Because this was in your heart, and you have not asked riches, wealth, honor, or the life of those who hate you, nor yet have you asked for long life; but have asked for wisdom and knowledge for yourself, that you may judge my people, over whom I have made you king, therefore wisdom and knowledge is granted to you. I will give you riches, wealth, and honor, such as none of the kings have had who have been before you, and none after you will have."

Perhaps that's the answer: it was Solomon's deal, not mine. I raised 3 boys that were not my own, and I asked for wisdom in raising them. I amazed their uncle, who did not think that I was the best man for the job. With that request, God granted me length of days. The rest has been mostly a struggle.

Ways of pleasantness and paths of peace? This may be mistranslated. Nowhere in God's Word, except for here, have I seen such an offer. Nowhere do I find that God offers us an easy stroll down a well-mown garden path. On the contrary. But He does offer to walk alongside us during our walk through life.

Psalm 23:4. Even though I walk through the valley of the shadow of death,
  I will fear no evil, for you are with me.
 Your rod and your staff,
  they comfort me.

Luke 24:13-15. Behold, two of them were going that very day to a village named Emmaus, which was sixty stadia [about 7 miles] from Jerusalem. They talked with each other about all of these things which had happened. While they talked and questioned together, Jesus himself came near, and went with them.

Hebrews 13:5b. "I will in no way leave you, neither will I in any way forsake you."

Prayer. Lord, thank You for sending Your Only Son to walk this walk of life ahead of us and to walk through life with us now. Teach us to trust You along the Way. Thank You, Lord. In Jesus' Name. Amen!

Proverbs 3:18

She is a tree of life to those who lay hold of her.
        Happy is everyone who retains her.

Wisdom, Day 11. Tree Of Life

Trees have always been a happy part of life for me. Growing up, I used to enjoy climbing trees. I would stand at the base of a tree, jump, grab ahold of the lowest branch, swing myself up into the tree, and begin climbing it, not stopping until I reached the very top of the tree. One of my funniest memories growing up was of my older brother chasing me across the yard. I spotted a pine tree, climbed up into it, and to my surprise my brother began climbing up into the tree after me; he was not much of a tree climber. I could hear him say from below me, "Oh, you've messed up now!" Up the tree he came, after me! Needing a desperate solution to my predicament, I chose to grab ahold of the very top of the tree and…jump! The tree bent over, like an upside down 'J' and lowered me slowly toward the ground. When I was about 2 feet off of the ground, I let go of the tree. I landed softly and safely on the ground. I ran back across the yard, stopping only briefly to look back at the tree. To my amusement, the tree was swinging violently back and forth, and my poor brother was hanging onto the tree for dear life! Wing, wing, wing! Oh, those were the days! My younger brother and I used to build treehouses in those trees; we had several of them. We and our friends would spend hours playing in them. They were such wonderful fun. I spent so much time playing in trees that when it was time for me to come in the house for dinner, my mother knew where to find me. She would open the back door to the house, holler my name, and call me in to dinner. Then she would get frustrated with how long it took me to get down out of whatever tree and run into the house. Whereupon, she would utter that famous phrase, "If you fall out of that tree and break your leg, don't you come running to me!" Don't worry, Ma, I won't.

Having grown up in New England, fall and trees were always a wonderful part of the year. We enjoyed viewing the beautiful fall foliage. We would drive on a Sunday afternoon after church, gas being cheap in those days, and look for the best view of fall foliage that we could find. It's no wonder that years later in the 1980s, while ministering in the National Parks, and in particular along the Blue Ridge Parkway in Virginia, I would enjoy driving along the parkway in October, stopping at overlooks and staring at the hillsides, taking in the beauty of all those fall colors. Oh, how beautiful is God's Creation, and the trees that He paints with vibrant colors in the autumn season of life!

The first trees that God created were in the Garden of Eden.

Genesis 2:9, 3:22. Out of the ground Yahweh God made every tree to grow that is pleasant to the sight, and good for food, including the tree of life in the middle of the garden and the tree of the knowledge of good and evil. Yahweh God said, "Behold, the man has become like one of us, knowing good and evil. Now, lest he reach out his hand, and also take of the tree of life, and eat, and live forever…"

Oh, the second part. If only they hadn't eaten of the fruit of that tree! We would live forever. Alas! But, did you know, that will all be restored?

Revelation 22:2. On this side of the river and on that was the tree of life, bearing twelve kinds of fruits, yielding its fruit every month. The leaves of the tree were for the healing of the nations.

What a dear and precious promise! One day! I look forward to that day. I shall hold onto the precious trees of my life and to that precious promise of that Day. For, as is Wisdom, Jesus is my Tree of Life.

Prayer. Father, thank You that You gave us Your Only Son, Who is the Tree of Life to those who take hold of Him. Teach us, Lord, to choose You and to remain in You, that we may be happy in You. In Jesus' Name. Amen!

Proverbs 4:1-13

1 Listen, sons, to a father's instruction.
    Pay attention and know understanding;
2 for I give you sound learning.
    Don't forsake my law.
3 For I was a son to my father,
    tender and an only child in the sight of my mother.
4 He taught me, and said to me:
    "Let your heart retain my words.
    Keep my commandments, and live.
5 Get wisdom.
    Get understanding.
    Don't forget, neither swerve from the words of my mouth.
6 Don't forsake her, and she will preserve you.
    Love her, and she will keep you.
7 Wisdom is supreme.
    Get wisdom.
    Yes, though it costs all your possessions, get understanding.
8 Esteem her, and she will exalt you.
    She will bring you to honor, when you embrace her.
9 She will give to your head a garland of grace.
    She will deliver a crown of splendor to you."
10 Listen, my son, and receive my sayings.
    The years of your life will be many.
11 I have taught you in the way of wisdom.
    I have led you in straight paths.
12 When you go, your steps will not be hampered.
    When you run, you will not stumble.
13 Take firm hold of instruction.
    Don't let her go. Keep her,
    for she is your life.

Wisdom, Day 12. Security In Wisdom

Get Jesus! I did not know until the age of 13 that I needed to have a personal relationship with Jesus. My parents went to church every Sunday and they brought me to Sunday school, along with my 2 brothers. I also attended a youth group at church on Sunday evening. We were always in church, every Sunday. If our family went away on vacation during the summer, we waited until after church on Sunday before we left and we returned on Saturday night, so that we could be at our own church on Sunday morning. We were always in church. I thought that was all that we needed. Then one Sunday night in youth group, 2 girls led the discussion and asked us all what would happen if we were in a car accident on the way home from church that night. If we died, where would we go? There were only 2 options, Heaven or Hell. Where would we spend eternity? I realized that I had never thought about that before. I was young. I did not know. They told us that if we believed that Jesus Christ died on the cross at Calvary to pay the penalty for our sins, rose from the dead on the third day, and ascended into Heaven, that we could be forgiven of our sins and we would go to Heaven when we died. They taught me about Jesus and gave me something to think about that night. Every summer the group went away on a week-long retreat and they asked me to go with them. I asked them what it was like. They said that it was like being in Heaven for a week, being with like-minded believers. I thought that sounded a little strange, but I liked these people and they seemed to be really happy. I didn't go that year, as I wasn't sure, but after they got back and told about what a wonderful time they had there, I knelt down beside my bed one night and prayed a real prayer to God in Heaven. I told Him that I was sorry that I didn't go with my friends, that I loved Him, I was sorry for my sins, I wanted forgiveness, and wanted what my friends had. I believed what they had told me, and I wanted Jesus in my life. I became a Christian that night, told my friends all about it the next Sunday, and went to the retreat with them the next summer. They were right! It was like being in Heaven, being with like-minded believers. It was a wonderful week. It went by all too quickly. Get Jesus! Do not forsake Him. He will keep you.

Psalm 41:2. Yahweh will preserve him, and keep him alive.
>He shall be blessed on the earth,
>and he will not surrender him to the will of his enemies.

Psalm 34:8. Oh taste and see that Yahweh is good.
>Blessed is the man who takes refuge in him.

John 18:9. (Jesus) "Of those whom you have given me, I have lost none."

Exalt Him! He will promote you.

Jeremiah 29:11. "For I know the thoughts that I think toward you," says Yahweh, "thoughts of peace, and not of evil, to give you hope and a future."

Prayer. Thank You, Lord, that You are our Protector, our Jehovah-Roi. Teach us to trust in You, to have a personal relationship with You, and to spend time with You each and every day. Thank You for Your love for us. Teach us to love You in return. In Jesus' Name. Amen!

Proverbs 4:14-18

14 Don't enter into the path of the wicked.
    Don't walk in the way of evil men.
15 Avoid it, and don't pass by it.
    Turn from it, and pass on.
16 For they don't sleep, unless they do evil.
    Their sleep is taken away, unless they make someone fall.
17 For they eat the bread of wickedness,
    and drink the wine of violence.
18 But the path of the righteous is like the dawning light,
    that shines more and more until the perfect day.

Wisdom, Day 13. Do Not Enter!

Just before the turn of the century, I was working for an ambulance company, and on one particular day I was transporting a patient to the airport in a non-emergent vehicle. As often happened, we did not have much time to get there, time enough to contend with congested traffic along the way. Apparently, I missed one of the direction signs to the airport and I found myself readjusting my route of travel, trying to correct for my error along the way. This was before the days of GPS and the advantage of "recalculating." Suddenly, I spotted an airport sign! Unfortunately, it read, "Emergency Route to Airport. Authorized Vehicles Only. Do Not Enter." My vehicle had a red stripe along the side of it, along with the name of the ambulance company, and time was getting short, so I took a chance and followed the emergency route. I encountered a checkpoint along the way and saw a uniformed police officer watching vehicles approaching the airport. I composed myself with my most professional look, sat up straight, waved to the officer, and pointed toward the airport. He gave both my vehicle and me a questionable look, but nodded and waved me on toward my destination. Whew! I got my patient to the airport on time and then returned. Fortunately, nothing further resulted from my misadventure.

"Do Not Enter" signs are there for our protection. Exit ramps depositing traffic off of highways onto secondary roads are guarded on the other end by white signs with a bright red ball in the middle of them, along with those words all in capital letters. Otherwise a confused motorist would encounter head-on traffic, resulting in disastrous consequences.

God told the Hebrew people not to go up the mountain.

Exodus 19:12. (Yahweh) "You shall set bounds to the people all around, saying, 'Be careful that you don't go up onto the mountain, or touch its border. Whoever touches the mountain shall be surely put to death…'"

After 12 spies explored the land of Canaan and then brought back a report, the people were discouraged, for fear of 'the giants' in the land, and refused to enter. God became angry with their lack of trust and spoke against them. They then had a change of heart, stated that they had sinned, and presumed to enter.

Numbers 14:42-45. (Moses) "Don't go up, for Yahweh isn't among you; that way you won't be struck down before your enemies." But they presumed to go up to the top of the mountain. Nevertheless, the ark of Yahweh's covenant and Moses didn't depart out of the camp. Then the Amalekites came down, and the Canaanites who lived in that mountain, and struck them and beat them down, even to Hormah.

Do Not Enter! Do not enter the path of the wicked. Or of Folly. Do not walk in the way of evil or travel upon it. Travel instead upon the path of the just. "The path of the righteous is like the dawning light that shines more and more until the perfect day." (**Proverbs 4:18**)

Prayer. Lord, teach us to be obedient to 'Do Not Enter.' May we listen and follow You only. May we go only where You would have us to go. Thank You that You open doors for us and that You keep doors closed that You would not have us to enter. Teach us to trust You in this. In Jesus' Name. Amen!

Proverbs 5:1-8

1 My son, pay attention to my wisdom.
    Turn your ear to my understanding:
2 that you may maintain discretion,
    that your lips may preserve knowledge.
3 For the lips of an adulteress drip honey.
    Her mouth is smoother than oil,
4 But in the end she is as bitter as wormwood,
    and as sharp as a two-edged sword.
5 Her feet go down to death.
    Her steps lead straight to Sheol.
6 She gives no thought to the way of life.
    Her ways are crooked, and she doesn't know it.
7 Now therefore, my sons, listen to me.
    Don't depart from the words of my mouth.
8 Remove your way far from her.
    Don't come near the door of her house.

Wisdom, Day 14. The Peril Of Sin

When my brothers and I were growing up, we lived on the rural side of a town that would later become a city. My earliest memory is of sitting on the back porch of our house with my older brother, watching a backhoe dig a hole in the ground for the septic tank. Our side of town was that rural. We had very few neighbors. We had plenty of yard in which to play, as well as unsettled property around us. There were several sandpits in our neighborhood, one of which was quite large and semi-active, in that there was sand sifting equipment there. We had many good, friendly neighbors whom we trusted. Our parents never told us not to go near anyone's house, but we were told, "Do. Not. Go. In. The. Sand. Pits!" The temptation was too much to resist! The large sandpit was a lot of fun in which to play. There was plenty of space to ride our bikes. There was usually even a pool of water in the middle of the sandpit, especially after a good rain. We loved to take our Golden Labrador Retriever Scampy there, let him loose from his leash, and let him run. Oh, what fun! On one particular day, my younger brother and I climbed up alongside the sand belt which took the sand up to the top of a tower. We were exploring and it was a grand adventure. Suddenly we heard a woman's voice hollering to us from a house, "Hey! Get down off of there and get out of there! Or I'm going to call the police! What are your names? I'm going to call your parents!" Apparently, she was the self-appointed sandpit sheriff. Her voice was very loud and booming. It carried throughout the sandpit and was very frightening to two young boys. We quickly scurried down off of there, jumped on our bikes, and made tracks. Anywhere but there! We knew nothing about staying away from anyone's house, but we sure knew to stay away from the sandpit! In retrospect, it was dangerous there. Sand is very unstable. It is that upon which we are not to build our house.

Matthew 7:26-27. (Jesus) "Everyone who hears these words of mine and doesn't do them will be like a foolish man who built his house on the sand. The rain came down, the floods came, and the winds blew and beat on that house; and it fell—and its fall was great."

We became afraid of that woman that day. We never actually saw her, but her booming voice sure put a fear within us! Stay away from her house!

Solomon's words to his son were well spoken. Solomon was the second son of what had begun as a forbidden relationship. David, his father, had gone up onto the roof of the house, when he should have been off at war, looked at Bathsheba bathing, opened the door, invited her to his house, and committed adultery with her. A pregnancy ensued and David attempted to cover up his sin. When Uriah, Bathsheba's husband, would have nothing to do with the cover up, David had Uriah killed and took Bathsheba as his wife. This displeased God and the death of their child resulted.

Do not go near the door of her house! Stay far from sin! Do not go near sin! Abstain even from the appearance of evil!

1 Thessalonians 5:22. Abstain from every form of evil.

Do not go near the door of the house. Do not open the door. Do not go in her house.

James 4:7. Be subject therefore to God. But resist the devil, and he will flee from you.

Prayer. Thank You, Lord, that You love us enough to set up boundaries for us for our own protection, not to spoil our fun. Teach us to respect them, Lord, and to be obedient to You. In Jesus' Name. Amen!

Proverbs 5:8-14

8 "Remove your way far from her.
    Don't come near the door of her house,
9 lest you give your honor to others,
    and your years to the cruel one;
10 lest strangers feast on your wealth,
    and your labors enrich another man's house.
11 You will groan at your latter end,
    when your flesh and your body are consumed,
12 and say, "How I have hated instruction,
    and my heart despised reproof;
13 I haven't obeyed the voice of my teachers,
    nor turned my ear to those who instructed me!
14 I have come to the brink of utter ruin,
    among the gathered assembly."

Wisdom, Day 15. Pay Attention!

The further I went in school, the harder I found it to pay attention in class. It wasn't that I did not want to learn. I did want to learn. I just found it increasingly difficult to pay attention in class, as the material became more and more difficult to understand and learn. At times my mind wandered. On one such occasion, a professor came to a climax in his point, asked a question, and then ended that question with my name. He expected an answer, a coherent answer. He suddenly had my attention! Somehow my mind found a rewind button and almost instantly replayed what he had been saying, along with his question, and even an amusing anecdote about the flat earth society. I quickly put it all together, formulated an intelligent response, and even reconnected it all with that same flat earth society. And somehow, I beat the buzzer on it all for a fantastic, 3-point, half-court shot, that went 'swoosh!' If he was impressed with my recovery, somehow, he constrained his enthusiasm. But I could tell that my classmates were impressed, and I paid closer attention for the remainder of the class period.

Pay attention to Jesus!

Isaiah 51:7a. "Listen to me, you who know righteousness,
    the people in whose heart is my law."

Keep your eyes on Jesus. When Peter did so, he was able to walk on water.

Matthew 14:28-30. Peter answered him and said, "Lord, if it is you, command me to come to you on the waters." He said, "Come!" Peter stepped down from the boat, and walked on the waters to come to Jesus. But when he saw that the wind was strong, he was afraid, and beginning to sink, he cried out, saying, "Lord, save me!"

The words of Jesus lead us safely along the paths of life. They are not there to make our lives difficult.

John 10:10b. (Jesus) "I came that they may have life, and may have it abundantly."

The path that we need to follow is narrow and at times it may be difficult to find. We need to pay attention to Jesus and allow Him to show us the path to follow.

Isaiah 2:3. Many peoples shall go and say,
    "Come, let's go up to the mountain of Yahweh,
    to the house of the God of Jacob;
    and he will teach us of his ways,
    and we will walk in his paths."
For the law shall go out of Zion,
    and Yahweh's word from Jerusalem.

This advice is easy to give; it may be more difficult to follow.

Proverbs 14:12 and 16:25. (Solomon) There is a way which seems right to a man,
                but in the end it leads to death.

This is so important that he stated it twice. Whenever God says something twice, pay attention!

John 6:68-69. Simon Peter answered him, "Lord, to whom would we go? You have the words of eternal life. We have come to believe and know that you are the Christ, the Son of the living God."

Pay attention to Jesus!

Prayer. Lord, teach us to pay attention to You, to follow You, to allow You to lead us, for in You is life. Teach us to keep our eyes firmly fixed upon You and to walk with You always. In Jesus' Name. Amen!

Proverbs 5:6, 9:13

5:6 She gives no thought to the way of life.
    Her ways are crooked, and she doesn't know it.
9:13 The foolish woman is loud,
    undisciplined, and knows nothing.

Wisdom, Day 16. Danger!

Oh, to be transported back in time, to the mid 1960s, and to have the advantage of that bubble-headed robot in that science fiction television show. You remember, don't you? Oh, to be warned that way, by a humorous robot, who waves its arms around wildly in the air, calls out your name, and proclaims, "Danger…danger!" That robot was always on it, with some sort of extraordinary sense, like that spider guy and his tingling sixth sense. And he was always right! And he always kept his charge out of harm's way. Amazing! Without that robot, his human companion may have wandered aimlessly through life, getting into all kinds of trouble, walking off of a cliff perhaps, or falling into some sort of a hole.

Imagine life without that sort of warning. That's what life would be like, following Folly. Her ways are unstable, and you do not know them! And what sort of a guide would she be? Demanding and complaining vigorously, all along the way. Oh, what trouble she would get us into during our journey! It might be adventurous for a time, but it certainly wouldn't be like that Christmas song.

Jingle Bells, jingle bells, jingle all the way! Oh, what fun it is to ride, in a one-horse open sleigh. Dashing through the snow, in a one-horse open sleigh, o'er the fields we go, laughing all the way! Bells on bob-tail ring, making spirits bright. What fun it is to ride and sing, a sleighing song tonight! Oh…

That would be a much tamer and enjoyable ride than one with Folly!

Oh, that rides through life such as Folly's would come with warning signs. I remember going to that wildly popular theme park down in the Sunshine State and considering riding that scary ride through a dark mountain, back in the late 1970s. There was a warning sign given to people who were subject to heart attacks, motion sickness, and the like, that this was not the ride for such people. I went on the ride anyway! I survived and kept my lunch, but I did not give it a second ride. My wild ride was more suited to the toad. And to singing about how small our world really is. Wasn't there a teacup ride, too?

Jesus warned us about such people as Folly.

Matthew 23:23-24. "Woe to you, scribes and Pharisees, hypocrites! For you tithe mint, dill, and cumin, and have left undone the weightier matters of the law: justice, mercy, and faith. But you ought to have done these, and not to have left the other undone. You blind guides, who strain out a gnat, and swallow a camel!"

Paul likewise became frustrated with God's chosen people, the Jews.

Romans 2:19-24. You yourself are a guide of the blind, a light to those who are in darkness, a corrector of the foolish, a teacher of babies, having in the law the form of knowledge and of the truth. You therefore who teach another, don't you teach yourself? You who preach that a man shouldn't steal, do you steal? You who say a man shouldn't commit adultery, do you commit adultery?…You who glory in the law, do you dishonor God by disobeying the law? For "the name of God is blasphemed among the Gentiles because of you."

Beware then of such as these!

Do not even ponder Folly's path of life! Stay far away from her, and from the Devil. Consider ourselves forewarned. Her ways are unstable. You do not know them. Danger! Danger! Do not ride this ride! Stay clear of Folly. Do not have anything to do with the Devil! Let's keep our door closed to him.

Prayer. Thank You, Father for this warning! Grant us Wisdom in these matters. Teach us to stay far away from the Devil and not leave either a door or a window open, even a crack. Lead us not into temptation, but deliver us from evil. For Yours alone is the Way to Salvation. Thank You, Lord. In Jesus' Name. Amen!

Proverbs 6:20-26

20 My son, keep your father's commandment,
 and don't forsake your mother's teaching.
21 Bind them continually on your heart.
 Tie them around your neck.
22 When you walk, it will lead you.
 When you sleep, it will watch over you.
 When you awake, it will talk with you.
23 For the commandment is a lamp,
 and the law is light.
 Reproofs of instruction are the way of life,
24 to keep you from the immoral woman,
 from the flattery of the wayward wife's tongue.
25 Don't lust after her beauty in your heart,
 neither let her captivate you with her eyelids.
26 For a prostitute reduces you to a piece of bread.
 The adulteress hunts for your precious life.

Wisdom, Day 17. Beware Of Folly!

One of the best things that I have to thank my parents for is bringing me to church every Sunday. Although they didn't read the Bible to me, or even give me one, they faithfully brought me to church every Sunday and made sure that I went to Sunday school, while they went upstairs to the sanctuary. It was in Sunday school that I learned the stories of the Bible and about God's great love for me. I was given a Bible of my own in my third grade Sunday school class, once I was old enough to read it on my own. The lessons that I learned in Sunday school rooted themselves in my heart. They became a part of me. I learned such things as the Ten Commandments, which taught me to love God, honor my parents, do not steal, and not to desire things which belong to other people. **Exodus 20.** I also learned to do unto others as I would want them to do unto me. **Luke 6:31.** These lessons stayed with me, prepared me for life, and kept me out of trouble. They led me in the right way to go and protected me along the way. They illuminated my path as I began my journey in life. I knew these things not because my parents taught them to me, but because they brought me to church faithfully, every Sunday.

My parents also taught me to come directly home after school, and later, after work, every day. I was allowed to participate in extra-curricular activities, such as Cub Scouts, Boy Scouts, and church youth group, but my dad always drove me there and back home again. I also went on the occasional outing with these groups, such as to a baseball game or on a weekend camping trip, but I always returned home afterwards. These practices kept me out of trouble. I kept my father's commands and the rules of my mother. They kept me away from the evil one. My parents trained me up in the way that I should go and when I got older, I did not depart from them.

Proverbs 22:6. Train up a child in the way he should go,
> and when he is old he will not depart from it.

This means that each child is unique, just like an archer's bow. Just as each bow pulls differently, each child has his own peculiar 'bend' or uniqueness. Each child needs to be taught and disciplined differently, according to their 'bend' or their uniqueness.

To this day, when I get out of work, I return home to my wife. I do not so much as go out, even just for ice cream, with a co-worker, especially if the person is a woman. I do not chase after the beauty of another woman, for it would surely endanger my marriage. These are lessons that I learned from my parents raising me properly.

Prayer. Lord, teach us to honor Your Word and to keep Your commandments, for they are light and protection unto us. Teach us, Lord, to stay away from the evil one and not to be lured in away from our walk with You. In Jesus' Name. Amen.

Proverbs 6:27-31

27 Can a man scoop fire into his lap,
  and his clothes not be burned?
28 Or can one walk on hot coals,
  and his feet not be scorched?
29 So is he who goes in to his neighbor's wife.
  Whoever touches her will not be unpunished.
30 Men don't despise a thief,
  if he steals to satisfy himself when he is hungry:
31 but if he is found, he shall restore seven times.
  He shall give all the wealth of his house.

Wisdom, Day 18. The Cost Of Sin With Folly

During my teenage years, I was actively involved with the Boy Scouts of America. I had been a Cub Scout before that, but now that I was older, I got to go on weekend camping trips. We had different camping sites: sometimes we would go to Cape Cod and camp along the Cape Cod Canal, other times we would camp in our own neighborhood, and once a year we would go to our reservation. We would set up our tents upon arrival and then build a campfire upon which to cook our meals. The weekends were an enjoyable time of camaraderie, honing our skills, and learning to cook on a campfire. When the weekend was over, we would break camp, pack up our belongings, and return home. I always returned home the same way, smelling of smoke! I would have to spend an afternoon washing my clothes, taking a long, hot bath, and cleaning my mess kit and utensils. Everything smelled of smoke! Nothing escaped the smell. We always returned home the same way.

On January 20, 2004, while I was listening to the second inaugural address of President George W. Bush, I received a call informing me that my house was on fire. Of course, I thought that it was a mistake. Certainly, it was not my house that was on fire! I thought that someone had seen the flames of my wood pellet stove, assumed that my house was on fire, and called the fire department. I was in no hurry to return home. Until I got there, I could comfort myself with the thought that it was not my house that was on fire. I found out differently upon my arrival. It was indeed my house! The front half had been completely burned by fire. The rest smelled of smoke! I spent the night at my parents' house and returned the next day to see what could be salvaged – nothing! It all smelled of smoke. Even my clothes in the back half of the house in my bedroom smelled hopelessly of smoke. I counted it all lost, reported it as such to my insurance company, and replaced it all. There was nothing that was salvageable!

So it is with he who goes in to Folly! He who commits adultery shall not be innocent. Such a sin is a capital offense, punishable by death – stoning, both the man and the woman. In **John 8**, the scribes and the Pharisees brought a woman before Jesus who was caught in the act of adultery and called for her stoning.

John 8:4-5. "Teacher, we found this woman in adultery, in the very act. Now in our law, Moses commanded us to stone such women."

The man was not presented, perhaps because he was either a scribe or a Pharisee. But the man was not meant to escape.

Deuteronomy 22:22. If a man is found lying with a woman married to a husband, then they shall both die, the man who lay with the woman and the woman. So you shall remove the evil from Israel.

Beware! Whoever touches another man's wife shall not be innocent!

The warning is clear. Beware of Folly! Do not go near her. Do not go in to her. You will be as burned! You will not be innocent! Choose Wisdom. Choose Jesus!

Prayer. Lord, thank You for this warning. Teach us to stay away from the immoral woman. Teach us to choose wisely. Teach us, Lord, to be obedient unto You and to follow You all the days of our lives. In Jesus' Name. Amen!

Proverbs 6:32-35

32 He who commits adultery with a woman is void of understanding.
　　He who does it destroys his own soul.
33 He will get wounds and dishonor.
　　His reproach will not be wiped away.
34 For jealousy arouses the fury of the husband.
　　He won't spare in the day of vengeance.
35 He won't regard any ransom,
　　neither will he rest content, though you give many gifts.

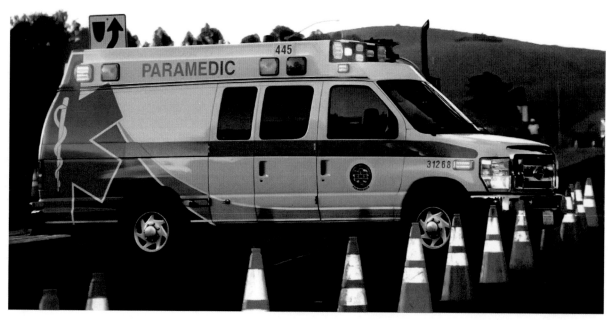

Wisdom, Day 19. Wrath Of A Jealous Husband

I am a retired Emergency Medical Technician. At the turn of the new millennium, I was working for a private ambulance company. A good deal of our work was transferring patients, both emergent and non-emergent, from one medical facility to another. On one particular day, our patient was the victim of a domestic dispute. He faced the wrath of a jealous husband and lost his battle. He was now fighting for his life. He had been beaten, almost unto death, and presented with a badly bruised black eye, among other injuries. It was not a pretty sight! He was a big man. I can't even imagine the size or the strength of the jealous, offended husband! My partner and I loaded him into our ambulance and proceeded with the transfer to another hospital. We were followed by a state police cruiser with flashing blue lights. We were successful with our transport and transferred the care of our patient to medical staff at the receiving hospital. We surrendered care and never learned of the fate of this man, although we presumed that his prognosis was not good. I would not even think about crossing either one of those men. I know enough not to offend them! I know enough not to commit adultery with a woman. I do not need divine intervention to tell me not to do so. However, I do appreciate the wisdom in the warning. Whoever commits adultery with a woman lacks understanding. He who does so destroys his own soul.

The second woman in our story is named Folly. We are here warned not to commit adultery with her. We are warned about the wrath of a husband's fury. We should remember from **Proverbs 2:17** that Folly left the companion of her youth and forgot the covenant of her God. Folly represents the Devil, or Satan. He does not seem to have a spouse. Our analogy breaks down here and cannot be extended this far. However, the Devil was once known as Lucifer, and as so, he was the crown prince of God's Creation of angels in Heaven. Unfortunately, Lucifer was not content with such an appointment, but chose to rebel against God and sought to set himself up as God in Heaven. God was having none of that and cast Lucifer out of Heaven and down to Earth as a fallen angel. In that sense, the Devil left the companion of his youth and sought out the children of God to drag them down with him into the very pits of Hell.

The angry husband is really God, the Husband of His people. By being unfaithful to Him, we incur His wrath upon ourselves. There is nothing that we can do to appease that wrath. There are no gifts to be given. There is no amount of pleading or begging. We are warned to stay away from the adulterous woman, Folly, or the Devil. The only recourse from having disobeyed is confession of our sin before God, trusting in His grace to forgive us of our sins and cleanse us in the blood of the Lamb.

1 John 1:9. If we confess our sins, he is faithful and righteous to forgive us the sins, and to cleanse us from all unrighteousness.

Did you notice that little word, just before the end? All! This isn't a Saturday sock wash. This is all!

He has promised in return to forgive us of our sins and to cleanse us from all unrighteousness. However, the better solution is to not commit adultery with Folly in the first place. Stay away from her! Do not go near the door of her house.

Prayer. Lord, thank you for this warning. Thank You that You love us so much that You warn us away from the very thing that will bring about our own destruction. Teach us, Lord, to understand that You know what is best for us, to listen to You, and to stay away from the Devil, his traps, his enticements, and his lies. Teach us to trust You and to be faithful to You, our Lord and our God, our Husband. In Jesus' Name I pray. Amen!

Proverbs 7:1-5

1 My son, keep my words.

Lay up my commandments within you.

2 Keep my commandments and live!

Guard my teaching as the apple of your eye.

3 Bind them on your fingers.

Write them on the tablet of your heart.

4 Tell wisdom, "You are my sister."

Call understanding your relative,

5 that they may keep you from the strange woman,

from the foreigner who flatters with her words.

Wisdom, Day 20. The Wiles Of Sin

When I was in 3rd grade, I found myself alone in a classroom. I opened the top drawer to the teacher's desk, and I found a quarter in it! At the time, that was big money to a 3rd grader. That was what I received for a weekly allowance from my dad. Being tempted by that quarter, I took it and put it in my pocket. I had a quarter! My joy only lasted through the end of the school day. While riding the bus on the way home, my conscience dealt with me. That was not my quarter, even though I had taken it. I knew that it was wrong. Once I got home, it became a very long night for me. I did not sleep very well, knowing that what I had done was wrong. I knew what I had to do! When I got to school the next day, I went right back to that classroom, found it empty again, opened the top drawer to the teacher's desk, put the quarter back, and…I put a nickel with it! Then I quickly left the room before anyone discovered what I had done. Somehow, I knew that was what I had to do. No one had ever taught me that. I had not told my parents and they had told me what to do. My heart told me that I had to put a nickel with the quarter when I put it back, to make restitution for my theft. That is God's law, the law of one fifth.

Leviticus 6:4-5. Then it shall be, if he has sinned, and is guilty, he shall restore that which he took by robbery…he shall restore it even in full, and shall add a fifth part more to it. He shall return it to him to whom it belongs in the day of his being found guilty.

How did I know that, even at the young age of 8 years old? God has written His law upon my heart.

Hebrews 10:16. "This is the covenant that I will make with them:
>'After those days,' says the Lord,
>'I will put my laws on their heart,
>I will also write them on their mind.'"

I fulfilled the requirement of the law that was written upon my heart by putting the quarter back and putting a nickel, or one fifth, with it. Once I had done that, I felt better and my conscience, or rather the Holy Spirit of God, had been satisfied, and I was no longer bothered by guilt. I had made things right with God and was forgiven for my theft. I fulfilled the requirement of God's law that had been written upon my heart. For the Old Testament Jew, God's law was actually literally carried around with them, at least a portion of it, bound or strapped to them in some fashion or form. It has now been written upon our hearts, by the very hand of God. We are to keep and obey God's law.

We are to say to God's Word, both the written Word and the Word of the Person of Jesus Christ, You are my friend. We are to be very familiar with the written Word, reading it daily, preferably by beginning our day by reading it and storing it up in our hearts. We may say to Jesus, "You are my Friend." That is not to say that He is to be our Best Bud or our BFF necessarily, but the Word calls Jesus "a Friend Who sticks closer than a brother" (**Proverbs 18:24**) and the old hymn tells and sings about "What A Friend We Have In Jesus."

What a friend we have in Jesus all our sins and griefs to bear. What a privilege to carry everything to God in prayer.

Treating the Word this way helps keep us from sin.

Proverbs 7:1. My son, keep my words.
>Lay up my commandments within you.

Prayer. Lord, teach us to keep Your Words and commandments and to be obedient unto You, for You have the Words of Life. Thank You for writing Your law upon our hearts. In Jesus' Name. Amen.

Proverbs 7:6-20

6 For at the window of my house,
  I looked out through my lattice.
7 I saw among the simple ones.
  I discerned among the youths a young man
  void of understanding,
8 passing through the street near her corner,
  he went the way to her house,
9 in the twilight, in the evening of the day,
  in the middle of the night and in the darkness.
10 Behold, there a woman met him with the attire
  of a prostitute,
  and with crafty intent.
11 She is loud and defiant.
  Her feet don't stay in her house.
12 Now she is in the streets, now in the squares,
  and lurking at every corner.
13 So she caught him, and kissed him.

With an impudent face she said to him:
14 "Sacrifices of peace offerings are with me.
  Today I have paid my vows.
15 Therefore I came out to meet you,
  To diligently seek your face,
  and I have found you.
16 I have spread my couch with carpets of tapestry,
  with striped cloths of the yarn of Egypt.
17 I have perfumed my bed with myrrh, aloes, and
  cinnamon.
18 Come, let's take our fill of loving until the
  morning.
  Let's solace ourselves with loving.
19 For my husband isn't at home.
  He has gone on a long journey.
20 He has taken a bag of money with him.
  He will come home at the full moon.

Wisdom, Day 21. The Wiles Of Folly

During my college years, I witnessed young men give in to Folly. We lived in gender-oriented dormitories. Men lived in men's dorms and women lived in women's dorms. The college had an 'in loco parentis' policy and it was against college rules for men to visit women in their dorm rooms and vice versa, except for on open house nights, and then under supervision by the head residents and expected good behavior. However, there were times when I was returning to my room that I witnessed a couple sneaking into a room together, looking around nervously, for fear of getting caught. These relationships often would not last and I would later see mementos being tossed off balconies or out of windows, only to smash on the ground below upon impact, symbolically ending a disastrous relationship.

Folly is not interested in a long-term relationship. Folly is only interested in an affair. Folly wants us to crash and burn. Folly wants to leave us broken and brokenhearted. Folly would have us see only the short-term pleasures of sin, enjoying the love until morning. Folly would have us believe that her husband is not at home and will be a long time in returning from a long journey.

The truth is that we do not belong to Folly. We belong to Wisdom. We are not our own; we have been bought with a price.

1 Corinthians 6:19-20, 7:23. You are not your own, for you were bought with a price. Don't become bondservants of men.

God sees us in our secret place.

John 1:48. Nathanael said to him, "How do you know me?"
Jesus answered him, "Before Philip called you, when you were under the fig tree, I saw you."
Jesus will return unexpectedly, "as a thief in the night."

1 Thessalonians 5:2. For you yourselves know well that the day of the Lord comes like a thief in the night.

2 Peter 3:10. The day of the Lord will come as a thief in the night.

Let us not give in to Folly's advances. We have a better offer than an affair, to be left broken and brokenhearted. Wisdom desires to give us a marriage, a wedding banquet, a celebration, and an eternity.

Matthew 22:4b. "Behold, I have prepared my dinner. My cattle and my fatlings are killed, and all things are ready. Come to the marriage feast!"

John 3:16b. (Jesus) "…whoever believes in him should not perish, but have eternal life."

Prayer. Thank You, Father, for Your great love for us, that You gave us Your Only Son, Who is even now preparing a place in Heaven for us for all eternity. Teach us, Lord, to wait upon You, to seek after You and You only. Teach us, Lord, to love You with all of our heart, soul, strength, and mind. In Jesus' Name. Amen.

Proverbs 7:1a, 5, 10, 16, 21

1a My son, keep my words

5 that they may keep you from the strange woman,
    from the foreigner who flatters with her words.

10 Behold, there a woman met him with the attire of a prostitute,
    and with crafty intent.

16 I have spread my couch with carpets of tapestry,
    with striped cloths of the yarn of Egypt.

21 With persuasive words, she led him astray.
    With the flattering of her lips, she seduced him.

Wisdom, Day 22. Beguile

Spring and summer are my favorite seasons. But they are difficult times of the year for men with wandering eyes. Coat season is over! People are dressing differently. And they seem to have a propensity for not wearing enough clothing. During the summers of 1981-1982, I ministered at Mammoth Cave National Park, in Kentucky. On Sunday mornings, I provided services of worship in the park's amphitheater, but during the week I worked a secular job, working for National Park Concessions. At first, I worked down in the cave in the Snowball Dining Room, providing food to visitors touring the cave. The temperature in the cave was a constant 56 degrees, so adequate clothing was not an issue. But later I worked for the hotel as a bellhop. At least one day a week I worked an early shift and it was my job to clean the lobby, including cleaning the vinyl covered sofas. It was not an easy task, as they were often very dirty. A woman who worked as a desk clerk used to watch me clean and would often comment that my task was made difficult by the fact that people did not wear enough clothing. The park was busy during the summer and many of the jobs were filled by college students, who were off from school for the summer. We lived in the park in dormitory style housing, segregated by gender. I was friends with a female park ranger, but we kept our relationship on a friendly basis only, meeting up for public activities only, and we always wore an adequate and appropriate amount of clothing. Being a park ranger, she had better housing than I did, but we did not meet at each other's housing. We kept our relationship public and appropriate.

Folly is not interested in a long-term relationship, but only in the moment. She is only interested in having an affair. She is all about crash and burn. She speaks seductively, flattering with her words, which are not sincere. She dresses seductively, wearing the clothing of a harlot, and is crafty with her words. Her bed comes up often in her talking and her words will paint a very pretty and appealing picture. But they are inappropriate talk and will come up prematurely in the relationship. They have no meaning, or any long-lasting or sincere intentions. Folly will soon lose interest and move on to her next exploit. For Folly, it is all about adventure and ruining lives.

Genesis tells us about a woman named Tamar, who played the harlot, putting on harlot's clothes and appealing in the open to Judah, having only a brief encounter with him and then going on her way.

Genesis 38:14-19. She took off of her the garments of her widowhood, and covered herself with her veil, and wrapped herself, and sat in the gate of Enaim, which is by the way to Timnah…he thought that she was a prostitute, for she had covered her face. He turned to her by the way…and came in to her…she arose, and went away, and put off her veil from her, and put on the garments of her widowhood.

In the New Testament:

John 8:4. "Teacher, we found this woman in adultery, in the very act."

Hebrews 13:4b. God will judge the sexually immoral and adulterers.

Beware of such as these! Beware of Folly and the ways of the Devil. These do not have our interests at heart, but only their own interests. They are not sincere; they are beguilers! They will lead us astray.

Prayer. Father, thank You that You created us as loving, caring human beings, with a heart to love others, and that You love us dearly. Teach us, Lord, to be faithful to You and to those whom we love. In Jesus' Name. Amen!

Proverbs 7:15-23

15 Therefore I came out to meet you,
    to diligently seek your face,
    and I have found you.
16 I have spread my couch with carpets of tapestry,
    with striped cloths of the yarn of Egypt.
17 I have perfumed my bed with myrrh, aloes, and cinnamon.
18 Come, let's take our fill of loving until the morning.
    Let's solace ourselves with loving.
19 For my husband isn't at home.
    He has gone on a long journey.
20 He has taken a bag of money with him.
    He will come home at the full moon."
21 With persuasive words, she led him astray.
    With the flattering of her lips, she seduced him.
22 He followed her immediately,
    as an ox goes to the slaughter,
    as a fool stepping into a noose.
23 Until an arrow strikes through his liver,
    as a bird hurries to the snare,
    and doesn't know that it will cost his life.

Wisdom, Day 23. The Appeal Of Folly

My wife and I acquired our dream house, one at a lake, soon after we were married. After several disappointing viewings of houses, we were on our way to our next viewing. Arriving in yet another lake neighborhood, we rounded a bend in the road, spotted a wonderful grassy lot with a picnic area, leading to a nice, sandy beach, with a dock and a diving float. We both thought at the same time, "We're home!" We toured the home, an older two-story house with 3 bedrooms, a large, wood paneled living room, and a nice fireplace. We liked what we saw and purchased our new home. However, our dream home soon turned into a big disappointment, yea, even a nightmare! We soon discovered that we had a leaky roof that needed to be replaced, even though we had been told that the roof had never leaked. We saw heavy rains one winter, beating down upon a frozen and impenetrable ground. The rain had no place to go and soon penetrated our house, which we had been told had never flooded. We hired a company that came out and removed the carpet and the sheet rock halfway up the walls. Mold followed. When the previous company declined to finish the job they had done halfway, we hired an environmental cleaning company to remedy the situation. When they pulled sheetrock off of the walls, they found another layer of moldy sheetrock underneath. The issues continued. We had been lied to and consequences soon followed, and the truth came out. Remedying these issues has been taking years.

So it is with Folly, for she does not speak the truth. Beware of one who says that she has found you. Beware of an offer with overwhelming details, seemingly too good to be true. They are! Beware of an offer that contains a bed! She mentions it, not once, but twice. Beware of an expiration date in an offer! Her offer is only good until morning. Beware of one who says that her husband is not at home, having gone on a long journey. Beware of an unexpected return!

Matthew 24:44. Therefore also be ready, for in an hour that you don't expect, the Son of Man will come.

1 Thessalonians 5:2. For you yourselves know well that the day of the Lord comes like a thief in the night.

Beware of one with enticing speech and flattering lips!

Proverbs 5:3. For the lips of an adulteress drip honey.
> Her mouth is smoother than oil.

In the end she is as bitter as wormwood and her steps go down to death. The end is prescribed. The fool did not know that it would cost him his life. Beware! Choose wisely. Let us choose for ourselves this day whom we will serve, Wisdom or Folly, Jesus or the Devil.

Joshua 24:15. If it seems evil to you to serve Yahweh, choose today whom you will serve…but as for me and my house, we will serve Yahweh.

Prayer. Lord, open our eyes, grant us Wisdom this day. Teach us to choose wisely. In Jesus' Name. Amen!

Proverbs 8:1-4, 10-12, 17

1 Doesn't wisdom cry out?

    Doesn't understanding raise her voice?

2 On the top of high places by the way,

    where the paths meet, she stands.

3 Beside the gates, at the entry of the city,

    at the entry doors, she cries aloud:

4 "I call to you men!

    I send my voice to the sons of mankind."

10 Receive my instruction rather than silver;

    knowledge rather than choice gold.

11 For wisdom is better than rubies.

    All the things that may be desired can't be compared to it.

12 "I, wisdom, have made prudence my dwelling.

    Find out knowledge and discretion."

17 I love those who love me.

    Those who seek me diligently will find me.

Wisdom, Day 24. The Excellence Of Wisdom

I climbed to the very top of Angels Landing, in Zion National Park in Utah, in May of 1982. I hiked the 2 and a half miles to the top, hiking up 1,488 feet along cliffs of sedimentary rock adorned with hardy pine trees and shrubbery. At times I climbed stone stairways and negotiated abrupt switchbacks called Walter's Wiggles, which made for a rugged climb. Once I got to the top, I rested and gazed down into the depths of the canyon and at the river below, watching in wonder as the rock walls changed in color from bright orange to deep browns with the setting sun. I gazed upon the vastness of it all and saw the hand of God upon its creation. I sat similarly upon the ridges of the Blue Ridge Parkway during the fall seasons of the early 1980s and looked upon the rich, vibrant colors of the autumn foliage. In it, the signature of the Creator of it all cried out to me!

Psalm 19:1-4a. The heavens declare the glory of God.
>The expanse shows his handiwork.
>Day after day they pour out speech,
>>and night after night they display knowledge.
>There is no speech nor language,
>>where their voice is not heard.
>Their voice has gone out through all the earth,
>>their words to the end of the world.

I invited Jesus into my heart at the age of thirteen. There He dwells, I with Him and He with me. I have never left Him, and He has never left me. Jesus loves me.

John 3:16. For God so loved the world, that he gave his one and only Son, that whoever believes in him should not perish, but have eternal life.

Jesus loves us all, as the beloved children's song states, "Jesus Loves Me" by Anna Bartlett Warner.

Jeremiah 29:13. You shall seek me, and find me, when you shall search for me with all your heart.

Prayer. Lord, I pray that we hear the voice of Jesus calling to us today, that we listen to His voice, seek Him with all of our heart, that we will choose Him, that we may dwell with Him and that He will dwell with us. In Jesus' Name. Amen.

Proverbs 8:34-35

34 Blessed is the man who hears me,
     watching daily at my gates,
     waiting at my door posts.
35 For whoever finds me, finds life,
     and will obtain favor from Yahweh.

Wisdom, Day 25. Going The Distance

I have been blessed late in life, having received not one, but two inheritances from family. I invested the first inheritance and later bought a house with it. I acquired possessions with the second inheritance, purchasing a bigger house on its own land, a 1960 Chrysler Windsor Golden Lion, and a John Deere lawn tractor. I have discovered, much to my dismay, that these possessions require daily care and regular maintenance. They do not take care of themselves; they require regular upkeep. Our house and property have required re-grading the yard, putting in a perimeter drain system, extricating tree limbs off the roof, repairing same, and cutting down storm damaged trees. The antique car required restoration and has required replacing, or rebuilding, the starter, radiator, and hoses. Currently it is sitting in its garage resting, awaiting the replacement of the battery and exhaust system. The lawn tractor has needed regular, annual, and often costly, maintenance. I have learned the importance of watching over my property and possessions daily, keeping watch at the posts of my doors. I appreciate these blessings in life and am learning how to keep up with it all.

So it is with the Christian life. Looking back at the beginning of it all, oh what a joy that beginning was to experience! However, it was only that – a beginning. The start of a journey. It was not the arrival of a privileged place in life without need of watching, maintenance, and improvement. One year after making my decision to accept Jesus Christ into my heart as my personal Lord and Savior, I made the decision to go into full-time Christian ministry. Fifteen years into my journey I became baptized in the Holy Spirit. Fifty years later I was ordained into ministry. My journey is an ever continuing one, requiring watching daily at the gates of life, at the posts of many doors. Those gates and doors need to remain closed and shut, not leaving them open even a crack, not allowing the enemy any opening into my life and my heart. This Christian walk is a race that must be run in order to win the prize.

1 Corinthians 9:24. Don't you know that those who run in a race all run, but one receives the prize? Run like that, that you may win.

Hebrews 12:1. Therefore, let us also, seeing we are surrounded by so great a cloud of witnesses, lay aside every weight and the sin which so easily entangles us, and let us run with perseverance the race that is set before us.

Our journey is not a coasting into the final reward of life, but one of daily watching and maintaining.

Matthew 24:42-44. Watch therefore, for you don't know in what hour your Lord comes. But know this, that if the master of the house had known in what watch of the night the thief was coming, he would have watched, and would not have allowed his house to be broken into. Therefore also be ready, for in an hour that you don't expect, the Son of Man will come.

Our watch is not an occasional and casual looking out the window, either. This must be a constant vigil!

Jeremiah 29:13. You shall seek me, and find me, when you shall search for me with all your heart.

Prayer. Thank You, Lord, for wooing us by Your Holy Spirit, for drawing us to Yourself, for purchasing our salvation through the shed blood of Jesus Christ on the cross of Calvary and His resurrection from the dead. Thank You, Lord, that You found us when we were lost. Teach us to seek You daily with all of our heart, to daily maintain our relationship and walk with You, and to love You with all of our heart. In Jesus' Name. Amen!

Proverbs 9:1-11

1 Wisdom has built her house.

    She has carved out her seven pillars.

2 She has prepared her meat.

    She has mixed her wine.

    She has also set her table.

3 She has sent out her maidens.

    She cries from the highest places of the city:

4 "Whoever is simple, let him turn in here!"

    As for him who is void of understanding, she says to him,

5 "Come, eat some of my bread,

    Drink some of the wine which I have mixed!

6 Leave your simple ways, and live.

    Walk in the way of understanding."

7 One who corrects a mocker invites insult.

    One who reproves a wicked man invites abuse.

8 Don't reprove a scoffer, lest he hate you.

    Reprove a wise person, and he will love you.

9 Instruct a wise person, and he will be still wiser.

    Teach a righteous person, and he will increase in learning.

10 The fear of Yahweh is the beginning of wisdom.

    The knowledge of the Holy One is understanding.

11 For by me your days will be multiplied.

    The years of your life will be increased.

Wisdom, Day 26. The Way of Wisdom

In April of 2006 I visited the National Cathedral in Washington, D.C. during the Cherry Blossom Festival. I went with some friends from college. We spent a week in our nation's capital, enjoying many other sights there as well. We spent most of a day touring the cathedral and were impressed with the architecture, the sheer size of the building, and the beauty of it all. It took 83 years and $65 million to build the cathedral, the sixth largest in the world and the second largest in the United States of America. There are 215 stained glass windows in the building, 288 angels on top of the 2 west towers, and 10,650 pipes in the Great Organ. The central tower houses both peal and carillon bells. Each year 400,000 visitors and worshippers come to visit the Cathedral. I left feeling truly amazed at the splendor and immensity of our country's national cathedral!

For about 2,000 years, our Lord, that Great Carpenter, has been building a much more impressive structure, a mansion in Heaven! In it are many rooms and a place for each one of us is being prepared. It is with great expectancy that I anticipate seeing this splendid mansion. I call it a mansion. The original language speaks of a family home with many abodes, or mansions therein. These words are rendered differently in various translations. The translation we are using says house and homes.

John 14:2. In my Father's house are many homes. If it weren't so, I would have told you. I am going to prepare a place for you.

By now, a careful reading of Proverbs should show us that we are given two choices. Two adversaries are competing for us and present us with two compelling offers. We are being sought by Wisdom and Folly, by Jesus and an adulterous woman, represented by the Devil. They are both inviting us into their houses. Jesus offers us a grand House that He has built. He has hewn out seven pillars for it, symbolizing perfection. His is a perfect House, Heaven. Compare **Proverbs 9:2.** He has prepared a banquet, the Marriage Supper of the Lamb. He has killed the fatted calf, mixed His wine, and has set His table.

Revelation 19:7. Let's rejoice and be exceedingly glad, and let's give the glory to him. For the wedding of the Lamb has come, and his wife has made herself ready.

We, the Church, are the bride of Christ and are being sought, wooed, and asked to make ourselves ready for this great celebration. The choice results in eternity with Jesus in Heaven. Any other choice is disastrous.

Proverbs 9:18. But he doesn't know that the departed spirits are there,
that [the foolish woman's] guests are in the depths of Sheol.

We are warned to choose carefully, for the stakes are high. Eternity awaits. Joshua warned so previously.

Joshua 24:15. Choose today whom you will serve…but as for me and my house, we will serve Yahweh.

Jesus asks us to choose as well.

John 6:66-67. Many of his disciples went back, and walked no more with him. Jesus said therefore to the twelve, "You don't also want to go away, do you?"

Prayer. Lord, thank You that You are preparing a place in Heaven for us and a banquet at Your table. Teach us to choose carefully in this life. Grant us wisdom to choose. Thank You, Lord. In Jesus' Name. Amen!

Proverbs 9:13-18

13 The foolish woman is loud,
    undisciplined, and knows nothing.
14 She sits at the door of her house,
    on a seat in the high places of the city,
15 to call to those who pass by,
    who go straight on their ways,
16 "Whoever is simple, let him turn in here."
    as for him who is void of understanding, she says to him,
17 "Stolen water is sweet.
    Food eaten in secret is pleasant."
18 But he doesn't know that the departed spirits are there,
    that her guests are in the depths of Sheol.

Wisdom, Day 27. The Way Of Folly

During my time in college, I took part in an annual January activity, during which a group of us would pack up and depart the campus for an almost month-long field trip. During this time, we would tour national parks throughout the country and camp out in tents each night. We would awaken the next morning, break camp, and head on to our next destination, usually another national park. A typical distraction during our routine was to take a day off from our travels after about 2 weeks and have a rest and relaxation day. One year we were in Louisiana, so we decided to tour Bourbon Street in New Orleans. Experiencing the night life of the city was an eye-opening experience! Hearing the jazz that sounded forth on every block was enjoyable, but the nearby distractions were quite the sight. Mingled there within would be best described as debauchery and dens of iniquity. Perched on the second floor of many buildings was a protruding display window. Within would be a scantily clad temptress, presenting her wares. At the door beneath would be another tempting woman, calling out to those passing by, "Come in and see! You won't go to Hell if you pass through these doors…" Indeed! Pass by I did, and quickly, so as not to complete my education and be corrupted by such denizens. Thankfully I survived our R&R and we proceeded to our next destination.

Notice that Folly is described as clamorous. She makes much noise! When a speaker has a weak point to offer, the trick is to make much noise about it, confusing the hearer. Folly sits at the door of her house on a seat at the highest places of the city, imitating Wisdom. She sets herself up as if upon a throne, as one who is important, inviting people who pass by to turn in to her. Her target is the simple, those who lack understanding. Notice her enticement. She calls out to those who pass by, as does Wisdom. She offers stolen water, and bread to be eaten in secret. What a saleswoman she must be to counter the offer of a mansion and a great wedding banquet with but bread and water, such as is offered as punishment to the disobedient in prison. Note that these are not normal, meager offerings; they are stolen water and bread eaten in secret, peddled as pleasant. 'Stolen waters' is a euphemism for adulterous sexual intercourse. There is pleasantry in sin, but for only a season, which is soon discovered. There is adventure and newness in such exploits, along with the thrill of avoiding being caught. However,

Numbers 32:23b. "Be sure your sin will find you out!"

Beware! The dead are there…her guests are in the depths of Hell!

Our suitors have presented their offers and they are both competing and compelling. Choose this day.

Job 34:2-4. Hear my words, you wise men.
>Give ear to me, you who have knowledge.
For the ear tries words,
>as the palate tastes food.
Let us choose for us that which is right.
>Let us know among ourselves what is good.

John 6:67-69. Jesus said therefore to the twelve disciples, "You don't also want to go away, do you?"

Simon Peter answered him, "Lord, to whom would we go? You have the words of eternal life. We have come to believe and know that you are the Christ, the Son of the living God."

Prayer. Lord, thank You for this urgent warning. Let us see the dangers of temptation and not turn in there, but choose carefully, seek after You, and follow You all of our lives. In Jesus' Name. Amen!

Proverbs 10:13-14

13 Wisdom is found on the lips of him who has discernment,
   but a rod is for the back of him who is void of understanding.
14 Wise men lay up knowledge,
   but the mouth of the foolish is near ruin.

Wisdom, Day 28. Consequences Of Our Choice

I worked in the national parks during summers and a sabbatical year I took off from college in the early 1980s. During one such time I worked at a national recreational area in Arizona. I worked as a gardener for the concessioner in the park, watering and pruning orange, grapefruit, and palm trees. A visitor pointed to a tree near me and asked, "What kind of tree is that?" Another person sarcastically said, "He's just the gardener. He doesn't know." I looked at the fruit that was hanging off of a branch on the tree and said, "This is a grapefruit tree." They both became embarrassed, either at their lack of knowledge or observation, or their attempt to embarrass me, and quickly moved along. I was blessed with an ability to think quickly on my feet and utilized that ability, both to my own advantage and sense of self-worth.

There are consequences to our choices and people will be able to know whom we have chosen to follow, Wisdom or Folly. Wisdom will be on the lips of the one who has chosen Wisdom. We will be known by the words that we speak.

Matthew 12:34b-35. For out of the abundance of the heart, the mouth speaks. The good man out of his good treasure brings out good things, and the evil man out of his evil treasure brings out evil things.

People of Wisdom also store up knowledge. People who choose Wisdom will have a desire to spend time in God's Word every day, reading it and storing it up in their hearts. Consider the example of Joseph in the Old Testament, who stored up grain in storehouses in Egypt, so that when it was needed there was plenty available.

Genesis 41:33-35. (Joseph) "Now therefore let Pharaoh look for a discreet and wise man, and set him over the land of Egypt. Let Pharaoh do this, and let him appoint overseers over the land, and take up the fifth part of the land of Egypt's produce in the seven plenteous years. Let them gather all the food of these good years that come, and store grain under the hand of Pharaoh for food in the cities, and let them keep it.

People who store up knowledge will then produce good fruit, which we will be able to see.

Luke 6:43. For there is no good tree that produces rotten fruit; nor again a rotten tree that produces good fruit.

Proverbs 18:20. A man's stomach is filled with the fruit of his mouth.
With the harvest of his lips he is satisfied.

Matthew 7:16. (Jesus) "By their fruits you will know them. Do you gather grapes from thorns, or figs from thistles?"

If we choose Wisdom, we will produce good fruit, people will notice, and will be attracted by that fruit.

What kind of words are found on our lips today? Words of Wisdom or Folly? How do we begin our day? By spending time in God's Word? Or do we rush out the door in a hurry, late for work, not having gotten up in time for devotions? The words that we speak throughout our day betray the choices that we make. By our fruits, by the words of our mouths, people will know us. There was a song that was popular in the 1970s, the words being repeated several times throughout the song, based on

John 13:35. (Jesus) "By this everyone will know that you are my disciples, if you have love for one another."

Prayer. Lord, remind us this day that there are consequences to our choices and people will know us by our choices, our actions, and the words that we speak. Teach us to choose wisely today. Teach us to begin each day by spending time with You, in Your Word, and in prayer with You. As we begin each day, may Your love so shine forth from within us that others may be attracted to You. In Jesus' Name. Amen!

Proverbs 11:12

One who despises his neighbor is void of wisdom,
but a man of understanding holds his peace.

Wisdom, Day 29. Love One Another

The property upon which my wife and I live has aging trees. We have oaks, pines, maples, and shagbark hickory trees in our yard. As trees age, as ours are doing, they become dangerous, drop dead branches on the ground during windstorms, and threaten to fall down onto the ground. The worst of these trees in our yard was an old pine tree that stood about 100 feet tall. Woodpeckers had riddled the tree full of holes, harvesting and eating whatever was living in the tree. My wagon and I kept busy for many years, picking up and carrying off piles of tree bark which had fallen off of the tree. A neighbor who lives across the street had spoken to us about the tree, as it stood at the edge of the property, well within range of falling upon power lines. After we made unfruitful attempts to have the power company or a tree company take down the tree, I spotted tree work being done in my next-door neighbor's yard. I called the number on the trucks and they came over when they were done and took down the dead pine tree, along with several other dangerous trees. I offered the wood from the trees to my neighbor across the street, who was glad to have it to burn in their fireplace. We have talked several times since then and we get along well with each other. I have always gotten along well with my neighbors. I have never had to build fences or walls along my property lines, in any of the many places where I have lived. I have always lived at peace with my neighbors and gotten along well with those who live near me.

Romans 12:18. If it is possible, as much as it is up to you, be at peace with all men.

Zechariah 8:16. (Yahweh) "These are the things that you shall do: speak every man the truth with his neighbor. Execute the judgment of truth and peace in your gates."

John 13:35. (Jesus) "By this everyone will know that you are my disciples, if you have love for one another."

These are the qualities that we should have within us as people of Wisdom, as children of God, as disciples of Jesus Christ. We are to live peaceably with our neighbors, loving one another. And who is our neighbor? Jesus answered that question very well, in a parable in **Luke 10**, teaching that everyone is our neighbor, including those who are in need and those who despise us. Let us follow Wisdom and live at peace with everyone, as much as it is possible and depends on us.

Prayer. Thank You Father, for sending Your only Son into this world. He walked among us, loved us, healed the sick, and even raised the dead. He taught us how to love one another. Teach us, Lord, to show Wisdom unto this world by enabling us to love as You love. In Jesus' Name. Amen!

Proverbs 12:8-11

8 A man shall be commended according to his wisdom,
    but he who has a warped mind shall be despised.
9 Better is he who is lightly esteemed, and has a servant,
    than he who honors himself and lacks bread.
10 A righteous man respects the life of his animal,
    but the tender mercies of the wicked are cruel.
11 He who tills his land shall have plenty of bread,
    but he who chases fantasies is void of understanding.

Wisdom, Day 30. Commendation

On April 14, 2019, I was presented with a Certificate of Ordination at my home church. This had been a life-long goal of mine and was finally achieved at the age of 62 years. Many other achievements had to come in place before this happened, such as having verifiable ministry in which I served. I had graduated from college in 1979, from seminary in 1984, and from hospital ministry training in 2004. But until 2019, I had always ministered under someone else's license, sitting in training under someone else's ministry, until I had been called by God unto a ministry that was all my own, waiting for God's perfect timing. I preached two sermons at my home church afterward, under my own license, and oh, how good and satisfying that felt! I had been commended, according to Wisdom. After a lifetime of service in ministry, I was finally granted what I had strived after all of my life! I have received few honors in my life, other than being an employee of the month on a few occasions and receiving a few diplomas. My special day in my life was my ordination.

Mankind has a basic desire to be commended, to be honored for an achievement. All of my life I have followed the Boston Red Sox, previously being a resident of Massachusetts. I had watched my team play World Series games in 1967, 1975, and 1986. They got my hopes up after a long, long drought of World Series titles, not having won the series since 1918. Then, finally, in 2004, I watched, often times on the edge of my seat, as my beloved team clinched the title, breaking "The Curse of the Bambino." I cried! We identify ourselves with our sports teams. When they win, we won! When they lose, they lost! We have a basic desire to be commended, to be recognized for an achievement.

1 Corinthians 9:24. Don't you know that those who run in a race all run, but one receives the prize? Run like that, that you may win.

Matthew 25:21a. His lord said to him, "Well done, good and faithful servant."

One day, one great and wonderful day, we will be commended by none other than our Lord and Savior Jesus Christ Himself, having run our race according to His Wisdom, and we will hear those long- anticipated words, "Well done, good and faithful servant." We are to seek not our own honor, but we are to seek to be commended according to God's Wisdom. He who is of a perverse heart will be despised and he who follows after Folly is devoid of understanding. But he who follows after Wisdom will be commended. Seek after Wisdom. Follow after Wisdom. Seek and follow Jesus, that one day we may hear those precious, precious words, "Well done, good and faithful servant!"

Prayer. Father God, thank You that You loved this world so much that You gave us Your only Son. Oh, how great is that love! Thank You, Father! Teach us to seek after You, to seek after Your Son and follow Him, and to share Your love with others, that one day we may hear, "Well done, my good and faithful servant." Thank You, Father! In Jesus' Name. Amen!

Proverbs 30:20

So is the way of an adulterous woman:
  she eats and wipes her mouth,
  and says, 'I have done nothing wrong.'

Wisdom, Day 31. Listen!

I was raised by two loving, Godly parents, who were regular church-goers and faithful members of our hometown church. They raised my two brothers and I in the best way they knew and produced three God-fearing, faithful churchgoing, family-oriented sons, a family who dearly loved one another. However, they never had "The Talk" with any one of us, to the best of my knowledge. The closest I ever got to that was when I was preparing to go off to college in Kentucky and become the first one in the family to leave home, go off on his own, and fend for himself. At some time before I left, I received a rather strange, in my opinion, talk from my mother. She attempted to inform me of the behavior, by that time's standards, of the people of the world, since I had lived in the bubble of family life up until that point and would soon be going off to live in a men's dormitory on a college campus. I was rather bewildered by what my mother attempted to describe. I looked at her wide-eyed as if she had 2 heads like that buzzard creature from the cartoons, finding myself disbelieving the story that she related to me. Surely, she can't be serious, I thought to myself. Such things as this don't really happen! I soon discovered that she was right, but hadn't even told me the half of it! Otherwise I received no instructions as to the facts of life, and was left to discover this on my own. By writing this devotional, I am urging parents to avoid this inadvertence and educate your children appropriately, and I am urging children to listen to what their parents have to say, avoid the pitfalls of life, and live a life that will be pleasing unto the Lord.

Scripture tells us that King Solomon had one son, Rehoboam (**1 Kings 11:43**), and daughters (**1 Kings 4:11, 15**). Proverbs was written by King Solomon, passing along parental wisdom to his children. This is significant, as King Solomon is the son of King David, who produced a son by an affair with Bathsheba, who was married to Uriah the Hittite (**2 Samuel 11**). David attempted to cover up the affair by summoning Uriah from the battlefield to spend a night at home with his wife Bathsheba. When Uriah refused, David ordered him into the heat of the battle, where he was killed. This displeased God so much that David and Bathsheba's son died as a result. There are consequences, even unto our children, for our sins.

Isaiah 59:2. But your iniquities have separated you and your God,
> and your sins have hidden his face from you,
> so that he will not hear.

David then married Bathsheba and had a son, whom he named Solomon. Solomon now wishes better for his children, especially his son. Solomon passes along wisdom he has gained, even by his own mistakes and the mistakes of his father, so that his children, and especially his son, would be spared the same troubles in life. Solomon is now having "The Talk" with his children, especially with his son, instructing him about the two types of women in life. He is also teaching his daughters how to be the right type of woman, a Godly woman. Solomon will ask his children eleven times to listen to his wisdom. (**Proverbs 1:33; 7:24; 8:6, 32, 34; 13:1; 17:4; 19:20, 27; 23:1, 22.**)

Prayer. Lord, I speak Wisdom upon us, upon myself in the writing of this devotional, and upon those who are reading it, that we will make wise, Godly decisions, choose carefully, allow You to lead us as we choose, that we may do so prayerfully, that the choices that we make may be guided by Your Wisdom, Lord, and not our own, and that You, Lord, would be pleased with the decisions we make as a result. May You be honored in all that we do. In Jesus' Precious Name I pray. Amen!

Proverbs 31:10-31

10 Who can find a worthy woman?
    For her price is far above rubies.
11 The heart of her husband trusts in her.
    He shall have no lack of gain.
12 She does him good, and not harm,
    all the days of her life.
13 She seeks wool and flax,
    and works eagerly with her hands.
14 She is like the merchant ships.
    She brings her bread from afar.
15 She rises also while it is yet night,
    gives food to her household,
    and portions for her servant girls.
16 She considers a field, and buys it.
    With the fruit of her hands, she plants a
    vineyard.
17 She arms her waist with strength,
    and makes her arms strong.
18 She perceives that her merchandise is profitable.
    Her lamp doesn't go out by night.
19 She lays her hands to the distaff,
    and her hands hold the spindle.
20 She opens her arms to the poor;
    yes, she extends her hands to the needy.

21 She is not afraid of the snow for her household;
    for all her household are clothed with scarlet.
22 She makes for herself carpets of tapestry.
    Her clothing is fine linen and purple.
23 Her husband is respected in the gates,
    when he sits among the elders of the land.
24 She makes linen garments and sells them,
    and delivers sashes to the merchant.
25 Strength and dignity are her clothing.
    She laughs at the time to come.
26 She opens her mouth with wisdom.
    Kind instruction is on her tongue.
27 She looks well to the ways of her household,
    and doesn't eat the bread of idleness.
28 Her children rise up and call her blessed.
    Her husband also praises her:
29 "Many women do noble things,
    but you excel them all."
30 Charm is deceitful, and beauty is vain;
    but a woman who fears Yahweh, she shall be
    praised.
31 Give her of the fruit of her hands!
    Let her works praise her in the gates!

Wisdom, Conclusion. The Virtuous Woman

This then, is the conclusion of the matter. This is the pearl for which to look. This is whom we are to instruct our sons to seek. This is the standard we are to teach to our daughters.

My search for such was long and arduous. I wish that my parents had so instructed me. I also wish that my own standards had been so high. Instead, my search was more like Jonah's search for a ship.

Jonah 1:3. He went down to Joppa, and found a ship.

The Hebrew language indicates a sense of ornament. In December we go out in search of a tree: a pine, spruce, or fir. We bring it home, set it up in a stand in our living room, put water in the stand, string lights around the branches, and hang…ornaments on the tree. Then we step back, admire our work, smile, and say, "I like it!" That's what Jonah was saying about the ship that he saw at Joppa, "I like this one!" And he paid his fare and went aboard the ship. How many decisions do we make the same way? Do we choose a car this way? I like this one! Or even a house? Or do we pray about our decision first? My search for a wife began as did Jonah's search for a ship. I like this one! And the results, like Jonah's, were disastrous! Finally, after getting tired of being treated badly, I cried out to God and said, "I want who You want for me!" Then, and only then, did God send me a **Proverbs 31** woman, a virtuous wife. We dated for many months, starting out slowly, then we courted, becoming serious about each other. Finally, I made my decision, and my move. We were attending SoulFest, New England's premiere Christian music event, a days-long, multi-artist, open air, continuous concert, held at Gunstock Mountain, in Gilford, New Hampshire. Towards the end of the event, we rode the chair lift up to the top of the mountain, to the Mountain Top stage. Then we rode the chair lift back down the mountain. While we were gazing upon the beautiful scenery, I leaned over and whispered those golden words into her ear. And…after an agonizingly long, 'deer in the headlights' stare…she said, "Yes!" We have been married for 12 wonderful years as of this writing! We've had our ups and our downs, our good times and bad times, we've had richer and poorer, sickness and health, but we are happy!

My advice is simple: don't settle for less than God's best. Don't necessarily take the first offer that comes along. Search for Wisdom. Stay clear of Folly! Ask God for Wisdom. Pray. Seek God. Hold out for the **Proverbs 31** woman, the virtuous wife. Let's instruct our sons to do the same. And let's raise and instruct our daughters to strive to be that woman. We are also to instruct our daughters that they should marry a man of God. Don't settle for "I like this one!" It is important to be physically attracted to the one whom we choose, and we are given the dignity of choosing for ourselves in our society, but ask God, "Who would You have me choose? Who is the woman that You have for me? God, I want who You want for me." See what God will do!

Proverbs 18:22. Whoever finds a wife finds a good thing,
    and obtains favor of Yahweh.

Matthew 19:5. (Jesus) "For this cause a man shall leave his father and mother, and shall be joined to his wife; and the two shall become one flesh."

Prayer. Thank You, Father, for this study in Proverbs. Thank You for sending and giving us Your Only Son. Thank You for giving us Wisdom! Teach us, Lord, to wait upon You, to seek who You want for us, and to teach our sons and daughters to do the same. Guide us by Your Holy Spirit I pray. In Jesus' Name. Amen!

May God bless you and guide you in your journey! In Jesus' Name. Amen!

ABOUT THE AUTHOR

John Harrison has a Bachelor of Arts degree in Religion, and a Master of Divinity degree. John is a chaplain, and he sings and is a teaching pastor at the church he and his wife Lynn attend. John and Lynn live at a lake, where John enjoys kayaking.

Made in the USA
Middletown, DE
17 January 2021